BEER HIKING
CHICAGO
AND BEYOND
THE TASTIEST WAY
TO DISCOVER THE WINDY CITY

Beer Hiking Chicago and Beyond
The Tastiest Way to Discover the Windy City

By: Jessica Sedgwick and Dan Ochwat

ISBN: 978-3-03964-033-1
Published by Helvetiq, Lausanne/Basel, Switzerland
Graphic Design and illustration: Daniel Malak, Jędrzej Malak (maps)
Printed in China
First Edition May 2024

www.helvetiq.com/us
www.facebook.com/helvetiq_usa
Instagram: @helvetiq_usa

helvetiq.com

MIX
Paper from
responsible sources
FSC® C167893

BEER HIKING
CHICAGO
AND BEYOND
THE TASTIEST WAY
TO DISCOVER THE WINDY CITY

TABLE OF CONTENTS

1

INTRODUCTION

ABOUT THE AUTHORS

So you want to know the secret to the 20-year marriage of Jessica Sedgwick and Dan Ochwat? Beers and hikes. Obviously there's more to it, but there is truth in the trail—you have to work together, communicate, and a boozy celebration at the end doesn't hurt.

Jessica is the navigator of the pair, getting them from Point A to Point B. Dan, well, he's better at getting from Pint 1 to Pint 2.

Professionally, they are Chicago-based media professionals and reside in the Lincoln Square neighborhood with their son Selden and blind dog Finn, who fittingly looks like the Lagunitas Brewing mascot.

Jessica is a marketing agency creative director, following a 20-plus career in magazines and newspapers, with roles such as Art Director for *Chicago* magazine, designer and writer at *Chicago Sun Times*, and more. She's also a former Girl Scout, which means her experience of getting lost on hikes started at a young age.

Dan is a full-time copywriter for a PR and content agency, and has also spent the majority of his career in journalism. Dan was a magazine editor and worked as a reporter for small newspapers. He also earned an MFA in screenwriting at Northwestern University, has optioned screenplays, and continues to write film, TV, and stage plays.

Together, Dan and Jessica share not only a love of storytelling, but a love of the outdoors and beer, something that merged during the COVID-19 pandemic lockdown. Needing to get the family out of the house, they set out to find the best hikes with nearby breweries. Most breweries are great places for kids, too, with musty board games and classic mac 'n' cheese. They're also perfectly acceptable locations to pull up looking sweaty—nobody can smell you among the tanks of barley and wort making music.

Jessica and Dan have lived in Chicago for more than 20 years and love exploring different neighborhoods of the city and surrounding suburbs. Dan is originally from the Northwest suburbs and Jessica from downstate Peoria, Ill., which gives them a wide perspective on all the best hiking and beer spots.

ABOUT BEER HIKING
IN CHICAGO AND BEYOND

Hot dogs with mustard (no ketchup), deep dish pizza, Willis Tower, Navy Pier, "the bean"—these are just a few of the things that typically come to mind when people think about Chicago. But this book isn't about those things. As passionate North Side Chicago residents of more than two decades, we wanted *Beer Hiking Chicago and Beyond* to use hiking and beer as a way to celebrate—and learn more about—the lesser-known parts of Chicago and its surrounding suburbs.

There's a unique history tied to each hike, as many of the areas this book guides you through were home to indigenous tribes only a few centuries years ago. The parks, as well as the breweries, are community connection points. Through a hike and a beer, you'll get a feel for each Chicago neighborhood's personality. And this is perhaps the most enjoyable part of the hike-and-a-beer experience: appreciating distinct communities.

From the artsy industrial taproom on the South Side of the city that we've paired with a lagoon walk to the tree-lined brewery in a resort-like suburb that we've paired with a deep-woods walk, the chapters of the book will take you through diverse parts of Chicago and beyond.

The Windy City is often described as being laid out like a quilt, with each neighborhood representing its own patch, stitched into the fabric of the greater city. This book aims to emulate this patchwork-like quality in its selections of greenspace and beer, extending out to the surrounding suburbs of Cook, Lake, Kane, DuPage, and Will Counties. We even thread our quilt out into Wisconsin, Michigan, and Indiana.

One thing that remains true across all 30 beer hikes is that a friendly wave of hello to a fellow hiker on a trail and a laugh over a good beer at a brewery goes a long way. Enjoying nature, simple pleasures, and human connection is what beer hiking is all about.

And while Chicago may be short on jaw-dropping mountain views and rolling green hills, the region provides quintessential Midwest hikes featuring beautiful prairie grass, streams and covered bridges, hilly climbs through dense oak forests, and plenty of fresh air and birdsong. Most of the hikes—minus a few urban hikes sprinkled in for fun—provide respite from fast-paced city life, and an appreciation of overlooked greenspace that's a short drive or train ride away.

The city and suburbs are not short on beer, either. As of 2022, there are more than 300 breweries in Illinois, which makes it the 13th biggest beer producer in the country, according to the Brewers Association. And more than half of those breweries are in Chicago. With hoppy and dank IPAs, experimental wine-fermented beers, surprising beer ingredients such as Jarritos soda, and plenty of classics like sours, stouts, and lagers, the Windy City's breweries run the gamut with what they offer. We recommend a flagship beer for each featured brewery—one we feel captures the essence of each paired hike—but there's something for everyone at these brewpubs.

CHOOSE THE BEER OR THE HIKE

HIKE LOCATION →

REGION →

MAP →

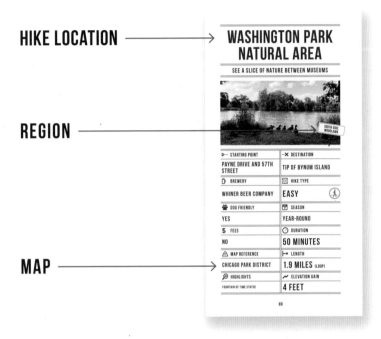

WASHINGTON PARK NATURAL AREA

SEE A SLICE OF NATURE BETWEEN MUSEUMS

SOUTH SIDE WOODLAWN

▷ STARTING POINT	✕ DESTINATION
PAYNE DRIVE AND 57TH STREET	TIP OF BYNUM ISLAND
BREWERY	HIKE TYPE
WHINER BEER COMPANY	EASY
DOG FRIENDLY	SEASON
YES	YEAR-ROUND
$ FEES	DURATION
NO	50 MINUTES
MAP REFERENCE	LENGTH
CHICAGO PARK DISTRICT	1.9 MILES (LOOP)
HIGHLIGHTS	ELEVATION GAIN
FOUNTAIN OF TIME STATUE	4 FEET

80

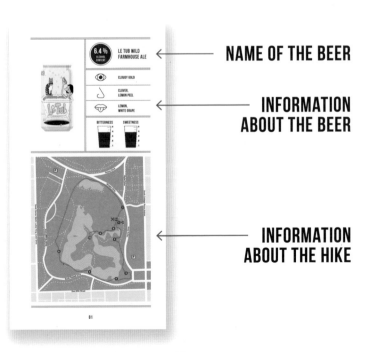

6.4% ALCOHOL CONTENT	LE TUB WILD FARMHOUSE ALE
◉	CLOUDY GOLD
👃	CLOVER, LEMON PEEL
👅	LEMON, WHITE GRAPE

BITTERNESS   SWEETNESS

← **NAME OF THE BEER**

← **INFORMATION ABOUT THE BEER**

← **INFORMATION ABOUT THE HIKE**

81

ON THE HIKES AND HIKE RATINGS

Each hike is labeled as "Easy," "Moderate," or "Difficult," and while much of the Midwest is made up of flat farming land, conjuring visions of effortless hikes through tall grass, the majority of the treks in this book include uneven terrain and inclines. We have tried to avoid paved paths and instead sought ways to extend hikes beyond the main loop, charting ways to get the most robust experience from each park.

Of course, no two hikers are the same, so what's easy for one may be moderate for another. The rough estimates of difficulty we provide are based primarily on mileage and the steepness and duration of inclines. Here's a closer look at the categories:

EASY

Under 3 miles long and with almost no elevation gain, easy hikes take an hour or less to complete and tend to be historical nature walks.

MODERATE

Moderate hikes tend to include rockier terrain and a bit of elevation gain. Most feature hilly climbs through forests and are 3 to 5 miles long. The paths are generally marked by visible tree roots and sometimes by fallen branches, so watch your step! The longer moderate hikes in this book can be somewhat taxing.

DIFFICULT

Only a few of the hikes fall under this category, including ones that feature sand dune climbs and distances of over 10 miles.

For each hike, we used a GPS mobile app to monitor the elevation gain and distance, and this data has been used to create the hike maps. Most of the hikes in this book are loop trails, meaning they begin at one trailhead, which they then circle back to. Some adventures include the option to follow noteworthy offshoot trails. There are also a few round-trip hikes, on which you return from your destination by retracing your steps; some lollipop loops; and some hikes that are combinations of two or more loops.

When it comes to directions to get to the trails, consider downtown Chicago as your starting point. Every city walk is reachable by public train or bus, and the relevant lines and routes are provided in the chapter descriptions. Of course, this may change slightly depending on where you leave from in the city. Parks in the suburbs come with directions to get you right to the trailhead, which may require a different route than just driving to the main parking lot or information center.

It's also worth noting, especially for hikers using map apps to drive to hikes, that each chapter contains information on the park system that manages the land—the addresses listed there are for that greater county forest preserve, *not* the location of the hike itself. The directions provided under "Find the Trailhead" detail the highways and exits to take to reach the start of each hike.

Almost every park is dog-friendly and can be visited free of charge. The hikes lead through park districts or county forest preserves that are open year-round (though Chicago winters sometimes beg to differ).

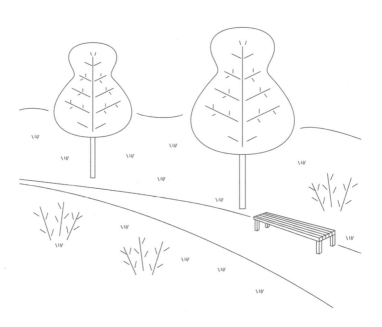

ON THE BREWERIES AND BEER RATINGS

With so many breweries throughout the Chicagoland area—and often more than one to choose from near each hiking location—proximity and a good story are what powered these pairings. Every brewery is fewer than 10 miles from the trailhead, and the majority are within 5 miles. Some of the finest breweries in Chicago did not make this book, but only because a worthy hike couldn't be found nearby. Which breweries to include may have been the toughest decision we faced throughout this process, but we felt it was important to find breweries as close as possible to each hike and to stay within the communities both served.

The beers featured in each chapter tend to be flagship brews that can be found on tap year-round, and we have tried to offer as many diverse styles as possible. The truth is Chicago is an IPA-heavy town. Every brewery has a standout IPA, whether it is a West Coast IPA, Hazy IPA, Cold IPA, Double Dry Hopped IPA, or Milkshake IPA—you name it. But they also have wonderful pilsners, lagers, sours, porters, and stouts, so we made sure to feature stalwart styles where we could.

Good breweries are always experimenting, and we witnessed many collaborating with one another on limited releases, which makes for a fun brewing community. Each selected beer has been rated on its bitterness and sourness and assigned an aroma and color. Of course, these descriptions and ratings are subject to the authors' tastes.

That's sort of the beautiful thing about beer, too. There's no *bad* beer. Not really. If you find yourself sipping a blueberry wheat ale that's a bit too fruit-forward to your liking, it'll still be a refreshing way to finish off a hike. But if you're worried about ordering something you'll wish you hadn't, you can always opt for a tasting flight, which is an excellent way to sip small pours (four or five at about 4 ounces) of various offerings to find the right beer for you.

The entertainment at the different taprooms varies: Some feature activities such as a pinball, foosball, or lively weekly Bingo, while others just focus on the beer. Food options also vary: Just over half of the establishments on this list serve delicious food, and the rest will either have a food truck on site or allow you to order in food from nearby restaurants.

City hikes are near public transportation, so the breweries are too. If you're driving, have a beer and hang around for an hour with some food. Drink water. Be responsible.

THE 10 ESSENTIALS (AND THEN SOME)

Even though Illinois and the Midwest is largely made up of flat, prairie grassland, it would be ill-advised to think a pair of tennis shoes and one water bottle will get you through the day. Hikers should wear proper hiking footwear, as the trails are uneven, rocky, gravelly, dusty, and often muddy. A change of shirt, socks, and clean tennis shoes is definitely a good idea, particularly in the spring and summer, when trails generally get a good soaking and you're likely to get wet and muddy. Here are some essential items to help make the hike both safer and much more enjoyable:

- **Tick Spray.** Before every hike, grab a can of mosquito and tick repellent and spray yourself all over. Don't just spray your arms in a short-sleeve shirt, for example. Spray the shirt. Spray the pants. Ticks are a real problem in this region, so don't underestimate them.
- **Suntan Lotion.** To avoid sunburn, a good sunscreen is required (we recommend at least SPF 30). Many hikes feature segments through open grassland, where the sun beats down on you pretty hard, so don't make the mistake of thinking you'll be mostly in the shade—even on hikes billed as forest excursions.
- **Hat.** For extra protection from ticks and the sun, we recommend hiking with a hat on. (And make sure you spray that hat with tick repellent.)
- **Bottled Water.** Hydration is hugely important when hiking, so have at least two bottles of water (or around 35 ounces) per person. Hydration packets are a good way to elevate hydration levels, so bring some with you on particularly hot days. You can pour them into your water bottle, shake it up, and you'll hydrate twice as fast as if you were drinking just water.
- **Snacks and Candy.** Just as hydration is important, it's also a good idea to bring trail mix or snacks to refuel on longer walks. While candy isn't essential, it *is* fun, and we enjoyed rewarding ourselves when we spotted a rare creature during a hike!
- **Map.** The maps in this book provide a helpful reference, but it's also a good idea to have your own map app open on a mobile device, or a printed map from the information center, as a backup. Just make sure to put that phone away while you're actually hiking so you don't miss anything.
- **First Aid.** Hiking through forests usually means coming away with a few scrapes and scratches from tree branches and thorns. Bandages and some antibacterial ointment are good to have on hand.
- **Hand Sanitizer.** To fight germs, especially between candy bites, bringing hand sanitizer on a hike is never a bad idea.
- **Poncho.** Those weather experts on TV aren't always right, so bring along a poncho (or other waterproof jacket) that folds up nicely into your backpack in case an unexpected storm hits.
- **Portable Phone Charger.** The map apps on mobile devices drain their power pretty quickly, so bring a portable charger that doesn't require a plug-in.

- ⚒ **Plant App.** There are apps you can use to identify and learn about plants, including whether they are poisonous. These apps only need you to take a picture of the plant in question and can be useful when walking through an area full of tall weeds and allergenic plants like poison ivy.
- ⚒ **Tools.** A small pocketknife can be a helpful multipurpose tool on a hike, including for removing burrs that get stuck to your clothes during wooded hikes.

Lastly, if you have access to some binoculars, bring them along, as they're a great way to see the hundreds of bird species in the region up close. There are deer, snakes, foxes, coyotes, raccoons, and many squirrels, rabbits, and chipmunks to peer at through binoculars, too. Hikes get you out into some great landscapes with lots of exciting wildlife, so keep your eyes peeled (just don't bother or approach the animals).

Being safe while hiking is also about respecting the land you're on. This includes not aggravating wildlife as well as staying on paths. Many of the hikes include some walking along steep cliffs, so there's no need to get too adventurous. Veering off paths also can impact the land that's being protected, so use your best judgment when choosing where to place your feet.

HIKING SEASON

A lot of these hikes are accessible year-round, as the forest preserves are also open during the winter months. Many are the site of sledding hills during snowy months, and state parks are a great place to go see frozen waterfalls. However, the ideal time to hike in the Chicago region is in summer. For reference, we completed most hikes between June and August, when Indian grass is beautifully tall, the weeds are overgrown, and the trees are bright and full. The summer months in Chicago can get very warm, so be prepared for the heat. That said, summer is generally still nicer than spring, when the great outdoors can feel very cold and dead. Of course, hiking in the fall is nice for views of the changing leaves, which go from green to rustic orange and red. Autumn hikes can get slippery, however, so take care when the leaves begin to fall and coat the trails.

HUNTING SEASONS

With the exception of one trail, every hike in this book is in a forest area or park on trails designated for hiking and biking, so hunting isn't a concern. For example, hunting and trapping are not allowed in any Chicago Park District or Lake County Forest Preserve. On the other hand, some locations, such as Starved Rock and Matthiessen State Park, have designated hunting areas in campgrounds far away from trails. Midewin Prairie *does* allow hunting in the fall and winter months, so wearing bright orange clothing could be good for that trail if hiking at that time. Different states and parks have different rules and designated months for hunting. Here are some references you can use to make sure you are being safe:

Illinois Department of Natural Resources
www.dnr.illinois.gov/hunting

Wisconsin Department of Natural Resources
www.dnr.wisconsin.gov/topic/Hunt

Michigan Department of Natural Resources
www.michigan.gov/dnr/things-to-do/hunting

Indiana Department of Natural Resources
www.in.gov/dnr/fish-and-wildlife/hunting-and-trapping/

Midewin National Tallgrass Prairie
www.fs.usda.gov/activity/midewin/recreation/hunting

WEATHER

Chicago was first called the Windy City as a slight against its blowhard politicians during the 1800s, but the city *does* get blustery winds off Lake Michigan. Any hikes near the lake can get chilly, particularly in fall, winter, and spring. Fall is a beautiful time to enjoy hikes through heavily wooded areas, as you'll see the changing colors of the leaves, but the weather can be fickle. Temperatures can be in the 50s with rain, but there will be the occasional day when they hit the mid-70s, so gauge the weather appropriately. Snowy winters can see temperatures fall below freezing, rendering most parks sledding or cross-country skiing destinations. And, unfortunately, early spring months can also be bitterly cold, with heavy rainfall. Summer is prime time and is generally characterized by blue skies and temperatures in the 80s and 90s.

Follow forecasts via the National Weather Service, www.weather.gov, or local news outlets.

ADDITIONAL RESOURCES

To learn more about hiking and breweries in Chicago and the surrounding areas, check out these helpful resources:

CHICAGO

Hiking: Chicago Park District, www.chicagoparkdistrict.com; Forest Preserves of Cook County, www.fpdcc.com

Breweries: Illinois Craft Brewers Guild, www.illinoisbeer.org; Malt Row, www.ravenswoodchicago.org/neighborhood/malt-row

Visitor Amenities: Choose Chicago, www.choosechicago.com

CHICAGO SUBURBS

Hiking: Lake County Forest Preserve, www.lcfpd.org
Kane County Forest Preserve District, www.kaneforest.com
DuPage County Forest Preserve District, www.dupageforest.org
Will County Forest Preserve District, www.reconnectwithnature.org

MILWAUKEE

Hiking: Milwaukee County Parks, www.county.milwaukee.gov

Breweries: Wisconsin Brewers Guild, www.wibrewersguild.com

Visitor Amenities: Visit Milwaukee, www.visitmilwaukee.org

INDIANA DUNES

Hiking: Indiana Dunes National Park Service, www.nps.gov/indu/index.htm

Breweries: Brewers of Indiana Guild, www.drinkin.beer

WARREN DUNES

Hiking: Michigan Department of Natural Resources, www.michigandnr.com/parksandtrails

Breweries: Michigan Brewers Guild: www.mibeer.com

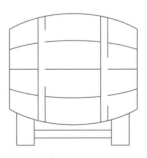

TRAIL ETIQUETTE

Proper and safe hiking starts with having respect for the trails and parks you're visiting. Chicago aims to provide parks, trails, and other outdoor-recreation locations that get people out and about and facilitate interacting with nature—smack dab in the middle of a bustling city. Unfortunately, city life can bleed into these parks, including in the form of garbage on the trails and graffiti. Please help keep the parks in good shape. Here are some basic guidelines to be mindful of when hiking:

- Don't litter. Use the garbage cans that are placed around the parks, or if you don't spot one, put the trash in your backpack. Hikers who litter parks with empty water bottles and snack wrappers are the greatest offenders of trail etiquette.
- Don't bring the noise. Hiking is a way to escape busy city life, so don't bring the noise with you to the trail. Don't blast music from your phone or a portable stereo as you walk the paths.
- Don't disturb the wildlife. Perhaps the greatest thrill when hiking in the Chicago region is seeing deer, chipmunks, cranes, heron, and other beautiful animals in the parks. After all, you're walking in their space, so be respectful, and don't feed them.
- Don't veer off the trail. Land managers and park officials go to great lengths to preserve the habitats and natural areas surrounding the trails. When directed to stay on a trail, please *do* stay on the trail. You may not know the harm you're doing to the plant life and ecology in the parks.

Hiking and getting a beer should be a communal experience, so it's also important to be friendly on the trails. Say hello to other hikers, move to the side to give them space to pass if you're going slowly, and always help if someone is in need.

Similarly, many of the hikes in the book are in dog-friendly parks. If hiking with a dog, be aware that not everyone likes your dog as much as you do. Restrain the dog until you get the go-ahead that the person you have encountered is comfortable with the dog. Also, remember to pick up your dog's poop. While you may think you're in nature and if the raccoons do it there, so can your dog, a dog's waste is filled with bacteria and parasites that are harmful to the natural local ecosystem. And the same goes for you! Please use the bathrooms at the parks.

Lastly, leave the park as you found it. The trees don't want your initials, and other hikers don't need to see them, so avoid carving these (or making any other territorial markings) along the way. Don't leave painted rocks, dolls, or objects on trails. We don't need to see love locks on bridges or fences or bumper stickers on park benches either.

Get out in nature to be with nature and other hikers, but don't leave anything behind except your footprints.

2

MAP & INDEX

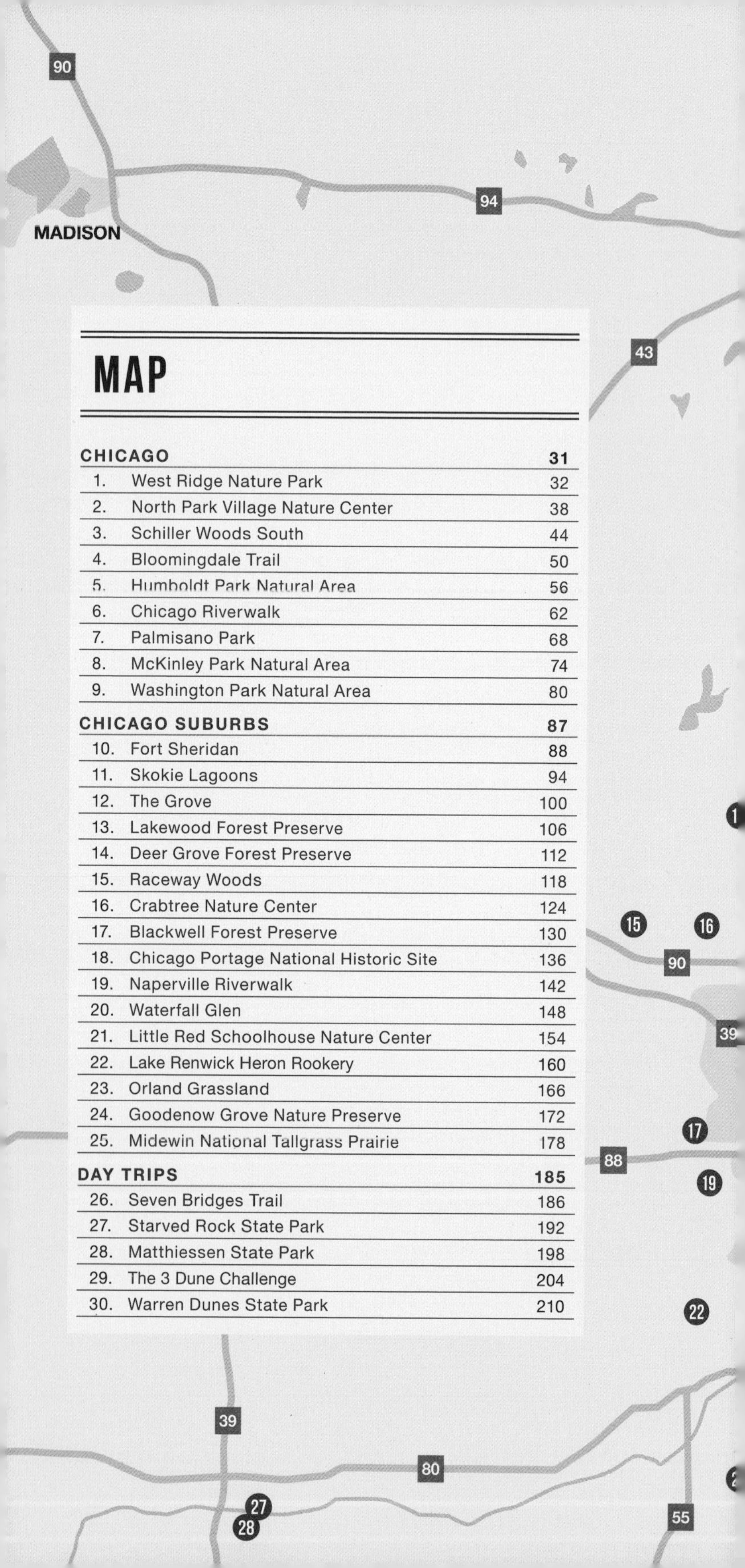

90

94

MADISON

43

MAP

1

15   16

90

39

17

88

19

22

39

80

27
28

55

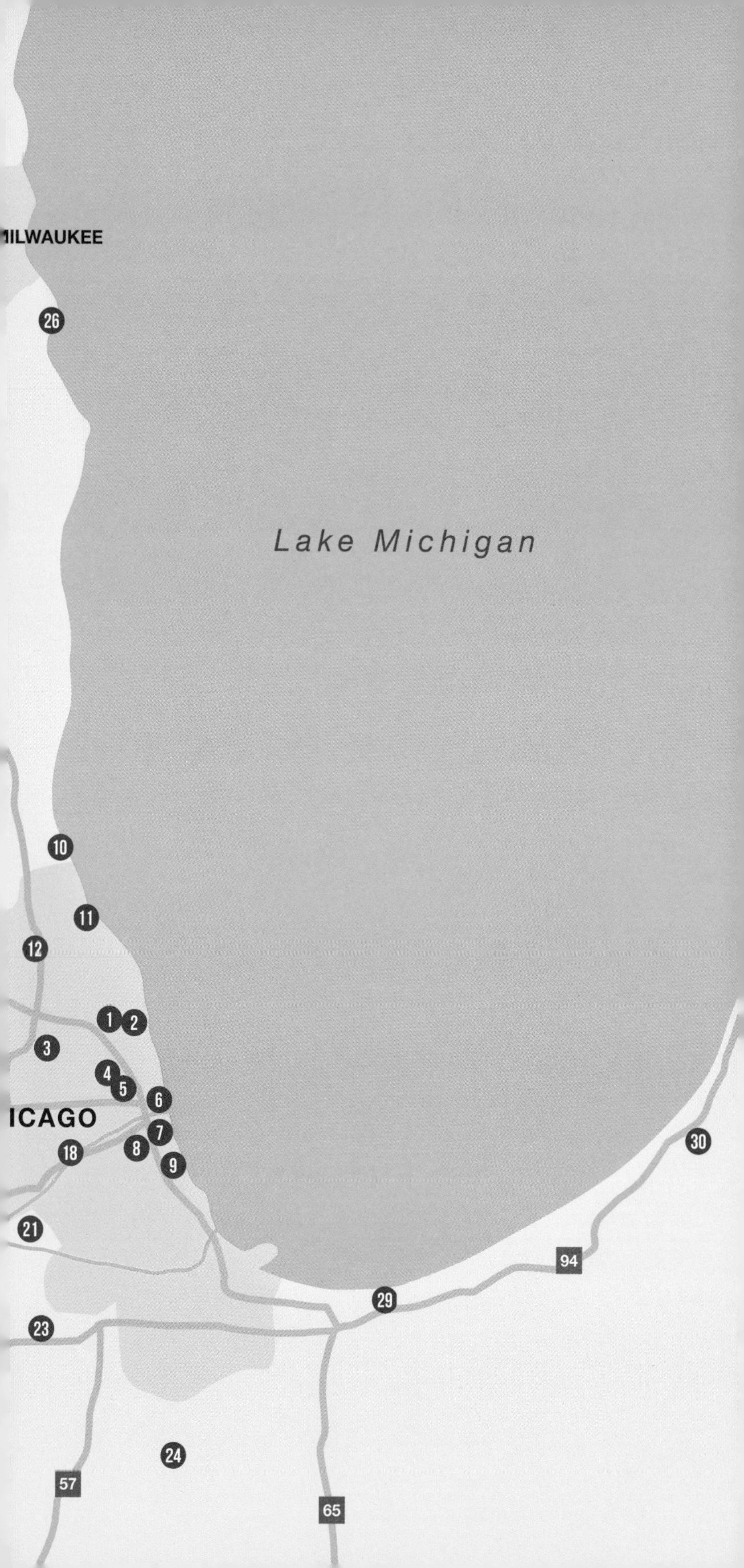

MILWAUKEE
26
Lake Michigan
10
11
12
1
2
3
4
5
6
ICAGO
7
8
18
9
30
21
94
29
23
24
57
65

INDEX OF HIKES

BREWERIES & BEERS

BREWERY	BEER	PAGE
Alarmist Brewing	Le Jus NEIPA	39
Black Horizon Brewing Co.	Key Lime Fistfight IPA	149
Broken Tee Brewing Co.	Beerantoni Italian Pilsner	89
Buckledown Brewing	Cactus Pants Mexican Lager	137
Buffalo Creek Brewing	Buffalo Gose	113
Bungalow By Middlebrow	Bungalow Lager	57
Chesterton Brewing Co.	Thin Red Line Blonde Ale	205
Chicago Brewhouse Riverwalk	Chicago Riverwalk Golden Ale	63
Duneyrr Fermenta	Sauvyn Blanc	69
Enlightened Brewery Co.	Kettle Logic Amber Ale	187
Evil Horse Brewing Co.	Lug Wrench Lager	173
Greenbush Brewing Co.	Sunspot Hefeweizen	211
Half Acre Beer Co.	Tome Pale Ale	33
Macushla Brewing Co.	Holla-Peno IPA	101
Marz Community Brewing Co.	Jungle Boogie Pale Wheat Ale	75
Obscurity Brewing At Lodi Tap House	Grape Pop Cultured Golden Ale	193
Orkenoy	French Pilsner	51
Phase Three Brewing Co.	Pixel Density Hazy IPA	107
Pollyanna Brewing	Eleanor Porter	155
Ravinia Brewing Co.	Diversey Station Pale Ale	95
Rt 66 Old School Brewing	Wildcat Cream Ale	179
Scorched Earth	Rugged Coalminer Porter	119
Short Fuse Brewing Co.	Loosey Juicy Hazy IPA	45
Solemn Oath Brewery	Snaggletooth Bandana IPA	143
Soundgrowler Brewing	Bike Shorts Grapefruit Radler	167
Tangled Roots Brewing Co.	Devil's Paint Box IPA	199
Two Brothers Artisan Brewing	Astro Fizz Sour	131
Werk Force Brewing Co.	Werktoberfest Marzen Lager	161
Whiner Beer Company	Le Tub Wild Farmhouse Ale	81
Wild Onion Brewery	Pineapple Misfit IPA	125

3

THE BEER HIKES

CHICAGO

WEST RIDGE NATURE PARK

AN URBAN OASIS WITH A PLAYFUL LITERARY THEME

FAR NORTH SIDE, WEST RIDGE,

▷⋯ STARTING POINT	⋯✕ DESTINATION
WESTERN AVENUE GATE	**STORYWALK PATH**
🍺 BREWERY	🔡 HIKE TYPE
HALF ACRE BEER CO.	**EASY**
🐾 DOG FRIENDLY	📅 SEASON
NO	**YEAR-ROUND**
$ FEES	🕐 DURATION
NO	**45 MINUTES**
△ MAP REFERENCE	↦ LENGTH
CHICAGO PARK DISTRICT	**1.3 MILES** (LOOP)
🔍 HIGHLIGHTS	〰 ELEVATION GAIN
SERENE POND, BOOK TOUR	**13 FEET**

TOME PALE ALE

 CLOUDY YELLOW

 CITRUS,
PINE

 CITRUS,
PEPPER

BITTERNESS	SWEETNESS
5 4 3 2 1	5 4 3 2 1

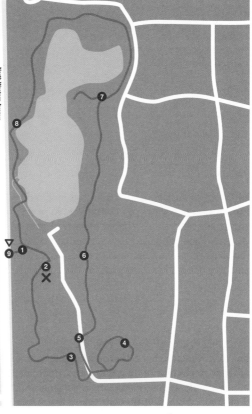

North Western Avenue

North Artesian Avenue

HIKE DESCRIPTION

Go for a peaceful walk and rediscover your inner child on the self-guided "StoryWalk" path. Continue the literary theme and curl up with a good book and a pint of Tome at Half Acre Beer Co.

Tucked between Chicago's longest street (the busy, 24-mile-long Western Avenue) and the largest cemetery in all of Illinois (Rosehill Cemetery), the Chicago Park District's West Ridge Nature Park offers a fun and surprisingly quiet jaunt that is ideal for hikers of all ages.

The tranquil loop weaves through 21 acres of woodland areas and grassy savannas, instantly transporting you away from city life. On summer afternoons, dozens of sunbathing turtles can be seen stretched out on logs and fallen trees in the shallow end of the 4.5-acre pond. You might also see the park's resident deer, and the preserve is perfect for birdwatching. Depending on the season, you can spot birds such as black-capped chickadees, a Cooper's hawk, Baltimore orioles, or red-bellied woodpeckers.

Built in 2015, West Ridge Nature Park has become the pride and joy of the neighborhood. After entering through the wrought-iron gate, you'll likely be greeted by a neighborhood volunteer who can answer any questions you may have about the park. The paved hike begins off to the right on the StoryWalk path.

Framed inside wooden signposts, a series of pages tell a story for you (and any children hiking with you) to read. The park changes the featured books regularly; some are old fables, while others tell educational stories about nature—for example, about the life of a newborn fawn.

About a quarter of a mile into the walk, you'll veer left off the StoryWalk and follow a circular path that leads to a stone resting spot and overlook for birdwatching. The offshoot winds back to a gravelly trail surrounded by tall black-eyed Susans that leads you back onto the storybook trail to continue your reading.

If you're hiking with children, look out for a rewarding play space on the right-hand side at the story's end. The space includes rows of tree stumps to hop along (ideal for a game of "the floor is lava"), rustic play kitchens mimicking cabin life, and even a wooden platform stage for young bards and poets.

After a look at the play space, you'll return to the paved path and begin a long walk around the pond. Short offshoot dirt paths lead to the shore for fishing and turtle seeking, and in among the trees, deer are often found feeding on the tall grass. This portion of the trail is adjacent to the famed Rosehill Cemetery, where some famous local historical figures rest—among them Oscar Mayer, Montgomery Ward, and Richard Sears.

The hike finishes by crossing a number of footbridges and following a paved path that circles the beautiful pond. As you wind back toward the entrance, the quiet of the oasis fades, and you'll be greeted by the hum and horns of Western Avenue traffic.

TURN-BY-TURN DIRECTIONS

1. From the park entrance, take the concrete path and bear right past colorful mosaic statues.
2. At 0.1 miles, bear right to begin the paved StoryWalk path.
3. At 0.2 miles, bear right to hop off the StoryWalk path for a quick detour. At an intersection with a gravel path, stay straight, then bear left to head up stone steps. Stay left to circle around to an overlook with a nice view of the woodland area.
4. At the overlook, follow the woodchip path that winds back down. Bear left on the paved trail. Bear right onto the gravel path.
5. At 0.3 miles, bear right onto the concrete trail to continue on the StoryWalk path.
6. At 0.4 miles, stop to climb around at the West Ridge Nature Play Space. Then continue around the concrete path that wraps around the pond.
7. At 0.6 miles, bear left and take a small wooden footbridge to another lookout point, this time with a pond view, then return back to the main paved path and follow it along the pond.
8. At 0.8 miles, take a rest at the fishing dock.
9. At 1.3 miles, arrive back at the park entrance on Western Avenue.

FIND THE TRAILHEAD

The West Ridge Nature Park entrance is at the intersection of Western Avenue and Ardmore Avenue. If travelling by public transportation, take the CTA Brown Line train to the Western station and transfer to the 49 Western Avenue bus to head North on Western. Exit at the Western and Ardmore stop.

HALF ACRE BEER CO.

Sitting in a quiet, residential neighborhood one mile south of West Ridge Nature Park, Half Acre is one of Chicago's most beloved breweries. It seems to add a new beer to its menu every few weeks, with a heavy concentration of IPAs. One of the best from its year-round lineup is Tome, a beautifully balanced hazy pale ale with both piney and light lemon notes. The brewers at Half Acre worked on different iterations of this beer—under different names—until they hit perfection with Tome. Half Acre is a gem in the middle of one of Chicago's greener parts of town. A bright blue neon sign welcomes you into the warm, remodeled taproom, accented by modern art and a clean design. The location offers a small but solid menu of bites, including one of the best cheeseburgers in Chicago. Outside is a large patio illuminated by twinkle lights, where you'll be greeted by a fun soundtrack of indie rock and soul.

LAND MANAGER

West Ridge Nature Park
5801 N. Western Avenue
Chicago, IL 60659
(312) 742-7529
www.chicagoparkdistrict.com/parks-facilities/west-ridge-natural-
area-park-park-no-568

BREWERY/RESTAURANT

Half Acre Beer Co.
2050 W. Balmoral Avenue
Chicago, IL 60625
(773) 754-8488
www.halfacrebeer.com

Distance from trailhead: 1.1 miles

NORTH PARK VILLAGE NATURE CENTER

WIND THROUGH THREE TYPES OF TRAILS

FAR NORTH SIDE, NORTH PARK

▷⋯ STARTING POINT	⋯✕ DESTINATION
INFORMATION CENTER	**WALKING STICK WOODS**
🍺 BREWERY	🗺 HIKE TYPE
ALARMIST BREWING	**EASY**
🐾 DOG FRIENDLY	📅 SEASON
NO	**YEAR-ROUND**
$ FEES	⏲ DURATION
NO	**1 HOUR**
⌂ MAP REFERENCE	↦ LENGTH
CHICAGO PARK DISTRICT	**2.3 MILES** (TWO LOOPS)
🔍 HIGHLIGHTS	〰 ELEVATION GAIN
PEACEFUL WALK IN BUSY CITY	**25 FEET**

6.0 %
ALCOHOL CONTENT

LE JUS NEIPA

 HAZY YELLOW

 TROPICAL

 TROPICAL, CITRUS

BITTERNESS

5
4
3
2
1

SWEETNESS

5
4
3
2
1

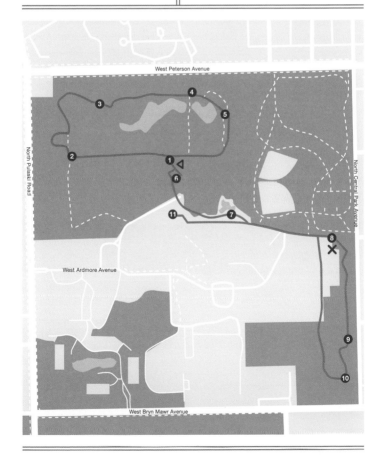

HIKE DESCRIPTION

Hike savanna, woodland, and wetland trails, and then find the secret Walking Stick Woods. Toast your discovery with a juicy pint of Le Jus at Alarmist.

The North Park Nature Center is a highlight of the North Park neighborhood and is located just a short distance from North Park University, a private university tucked along the Chicago River. An educational institution in its own right, the 46-acre nature preserve is home to a learning center with programs for children and adults, including nature summer camps and educational ecological restoration efforts.

The hike begins just behind the Information Center near a bird-watching hut. You'll steer left and onto the Main Loop, heading down a dusty path through tall grass, surrounded by gorgeous trees. The trail is the main vein, which you'll combine with the Woodland Trail and the Wetland Trail to create a larger loop trail. The Main Loop takes you through an oak savanna forest before joining up with the Woodland Trail.

The tree coverage of the wooded area eventually gives way to blue sky and tall prairie grass, a sign you're on the Wetland Trail, home to a beautiful pond and loud bullfrogs. A bench overlooks a pond, where you'll see water lilies and wetland grass sprawling out of the murky water. You'll then pass over a narrow footbridge, cutting through marsh grass, willows, and cattails. Next, over the bridge, you'll climb a hill of wooden steps to reach another beautiful overlook of the pond and the full nature preserve—a sanctuary in the city. Once down the hill, you'll follow a path that winds back to the Main Loop trail and the Information Center. But you're not done yet!

When you exit back to the parking lot, stay left along a wooded picnic area, which borders another pond with a man-made waterfall. This is the North Park Village Rock Garden, an ideal place for a brief respite. If you feel so inclined, you can walk over rocks and along paths up near the waterfall for a short adventure, but then head back to the street and toward the hidden Walking Stick Woods, a second woodland experience on the campus.

Along the street, you'll pass fields and the Peterson Park field house on one side and an industrial park district plant on the other. In between them, a small sign will appear next to a slight opening in the trees. This is Walking Stick Woods. You'll immediately be greeted by a rugged

nature play area with a little wooden lookout and huts made of fallen branches. Just beyond the play area begins a quiet, secretive-feeling lollipop-loop trail in the woods. This is like a speakeasy trail for beer hikers.

To get to the lollipop trail, you'll follow a short cobblestone walkway surrounded by beds of white snakeroot. This is the stick of the lollipop that leads to the circular head, a tight path circling through wild grass and goldenrods. Two random wooden chairs, about six feet tall, over-look the lollipop prairie grass and goldenrods, offering great views and a fun photo opportunity. The path eventually circles you back out to the street. You'll walk back the way you came and reach the parking lot. Next up, a beer at Alarmist.

TURN-BY-TURN DIRECTIONS

1. At the trailhead behind the Information Center, bear left onto the Main Loop.
2. At 0.3 miles, bear right to join the Woodland Trail.
3. At 0.4 miles, stay straight to get back onto the Main Loop.
4. At 0.6 miles, stay straight to join the Wetland Trail.
5. At 0.7 miles, take the steps up to the highest point for a view of the wetlands, then rejoin the Wetland Trail that loops around back to the Trailhead and Information Center.
6. At 0.9 miles, head past the Information Center and the Nature Center Parking Lot and bear left onto the North Park Village Road for the second half of this hike in Walking Stick Woods.
7. At 1.1 miles, for an extra adventure, stop at the pond to look for wildlife, climb rocks, and see a man-made waterfall. Then continue on the main road.
8. At 1.4 miles, at the Walking Stick Woods sign, stay straight to begin the trail.
9. At 1.8 miles, stay left.
10. At 2.0 miles, at an open field, climb atop one of two tall wooden chairs for an impressive view. Then continue back on the loop trail that will take you back to the main road. Bear left at the park road to get back to the Nature Center parking lot and Information Center.
11. At 2.3 miles, arrive back at the parking lot.

FIND THE TRAILHEAD

The North Park Nature Center is located at the intersection of Pulaski Avenue and Ardmore Avenue. If travelling by public transportation, take the CTA Blue Line train to the Irving Park station and transfer to the 53 Pulaski bus to head north on Pulaski. Exit at the Pulaski and Ardmore stop. At the entrance to the North Park Village Campus on Ardmore, head straight and take a left on an unmarked road just past the Gymnastics Center. Follow this road for 0.2 miles to reach the Nature Center parking lot.

ALARMIST BREWING

Brightly marked by its sign of a glowing neon stick of dynamite, Alarmist Brewing is a small brewery in a business plaza that packs a big punch. Le Jus, its flagship IPA, bursts with explosive flavor. The juicy, hazy taste is refreshing but still hop-heavy, and the beer earned a gold medal at the 2018 Great American Beer Festival. The brewery often adds seasonal spins of Le Jus, such as one with pumpkin spice for fall. The sun-drenched taproom has a neighborhood-bar feel, and there is a quaint patio out back. No need to sound the alarm (or light the dynamite), the brewery is the perfect place to relax after a hike.

LAND MANAGER

North Park Village Nature Center
5801 N. Pulaski Road
Chicago, IL 60646
(312) 742-7529
www.chicagoparkdistrict.com/parks-facilities/north-park-village-nature-center

BREWERY/RESTAURANT

Alarmist Brewing
4055 W. Peterson Avenue
Chicago, IL 60646
(773) 681-0877
www.alarmistbrewing.com

Distance from trailhead: 0.6 miles

SCHILLER WOODS SOUTH

HIKE ALONG THE RIVER AND THROUGH THE WOODS

NORTH SIDE,
SCHILLER WOODS

▷··· STARTING POINT	···✗ DESTINATION
SCHILLER WOODS SOUTH PARKING LOT	**WOODLAND TRAIL**
🍺 BREWERY	HIKE TYPE
SHORT FUSE BREWING CO.	**EASY** 🚶
🐾 DOG FRIENDLY	📅 SEASON
YES	**YEAR-ROUND**
$ FEES	🕐 DURATION
NO	**45 MINUTES**
⛰ MAP REFERENCE	↦ LENGTH
FOREST PRESERVES OF COOK COUNTY	**2.2 MILES** (LOLLIPOP LOOP)
🔍 HIGHLIGHTS	〰 ELEVATION GAIN
RIVER VIEWS, DIRT TRAILS	**3 FEET**

6.4 %
ALCOHOL
CONTENT

LOOSEY JUICY
HAZY IPA

CLOUDY MAIZE

CLOVES,
MANGO

PAPAYA,
STONE FRUIT

BITTERNESS	SWEETNESS

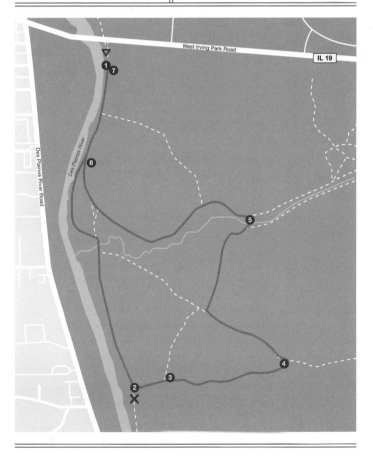

HIKE DESCRIPTION

Hike along the Des Plaines River Trail and then loop through the woods on a small, unmarked dirt path. Follow up your forest walk with a beer and some delicious pub fare at Short Fuse.

Schiller Woods is more than 280 acres of forest preserve right on the border between Chicago and the suburb of Schiller Park (in fact, you'll weave in and out of the city limits as you explore the preserve). The preserve is divided into Schiller Woods East, West, and South, and includes dozens of picnic groves, a sledding hill, fishing pond, and model airplane flying field. The park is especially worth visiting during the colder months, as herds of hungry deer congregate in the grass at the edges of the road and parking lot. (Note: Feeding wildlife is not recommended, even though this seems to be a thing here.)

Like many forest preserve websites, the Forest Preserves of Cook County's does not include smaller dirt hiking trails on its maps, which can make it difficult to find them. Despite the less-than-ideal signage, Schiller Park South is worth exploring. On this hike, you'll stroll along part of the Des Plaines River Trail (a 54-mile bike route that travels through most of Lake County and some of Cook County) and then duck into the woods for some fun smaller trails that feel more like true hiking.

From the Schiller Woods South parking lot, you'll walk south and away from Irving Park Road on the Des Plaines River Trail. At 133 miles, the Des Plaines River is the longest waterway in the Chicago area, running north to Wisconsin and south to join the Illinois River and eventually the Mississippi River. In the 1600s, local Native Americans showed early European colonists how to traverse the river to travel from Lake Michigan to the mighty Mississippi.

As you follow the trail along the Des Plaines River, you'll experience the impressively wide waterway close-up. You'll have your choice of staying on the wider unpaved bike trail or walking closer to the river, where you might find adventurers climbing on fallen tree trunks or looking for frogs and turtles in the river.

Not long after you start walking, you'll see an opening in the woods on your left for a small hiking trail, and then a second one shortly after; pass both and continue walking south for a little while.

This part of the walk is exceptionally picturesque, with the river and gorgeous woods on either side of the trail. About a mile in, you'll see a third unmarked trail opening in the forest on your left. Take this trail to head in under the trees for a little peace and quiet.

This wooded area is gorgeous in any season, but we recommend exploring it in the fall. The flat and windy path is surrounded by Japanese Bayberry, which in autumn carpets the forest floor with a vibrant gradient of gorgeous yellow, orange, red, and purple hues.

This trail butts up against the Indian Boundary Golf Course to the south, but still feels remote and serene. A mile and a half in, bear left to continue the loop back through the woods; you'll soon find yourself back on the Des Plaines River Trail, which you can follow northward back to where you started.

TURN-BY-TURN DIRECTIONS

1. At the Schiller Woods South parking lot, begin the hike by walking south on the wide, unpaved Des Plaines River Trail; follow the trail past two small, unmarked dirt trails on the left.
2. At 0.8 miles, bear left onto the third small, unmarked hiking trail.
3. At 0.9, stay straight to continue the loop.
4. At 1.3 miles, bear left to stay on the loop.
5. At 1.6 miles, cross a bridge and bear left.
6. At 2.0 miles, bear right to rejoin the Des Plaines River Trail and head north toward the parking lot.
7. At 2.2 miles, return to the parking lot.

FIND THE TRAILHEAD

The Schiller Woods South parking lot sits on the south side of Irving Park Road, one block East of Des Plaines River Road. Via public transportation, take the CTA Blue to the Rosemont stop and transfer to the 332 Cargo Road/Delta Cargo bus, taking it 8 stops and getting off at the River Road and Lawrence Avenue stop. Walk 1.3 miles south on River Road, take a left on Irving Park, and the parking lot will be just over the river and on your right.

SHORT FUSE BREWING COMPANY

After a lovely stroll in the woods, there's no reason to have a short fuse, so get ready to be in a good mood as you enter this colorful, spacious 7,500-square-foot taproom and restaurant (where they also brew and can beer). The name Short Fuse is represented in the taproom's decor—the walls are adorned with floor-to-ceiling murals that feature, well, people blowing stuff up (the style of the artwork is somewhere between video game art and war propaganda posters). Once you've checked out the murals and settled in, we suggest ordering the Loosey Juicy, one of the brewery's staples that was introduced in 2017 as their

first attempt at a hazy. With heavy notes of stone fruit, it's a bit more tropical than your average hazy IPA and pairs nicely with a salted Bavarian pretzel and beer cheese. If you happen to be with a non-beer drinker, the brewery has a line of spirits and a cocktail menu, but it is big on brew: There are more than 20 beers on draft. The popular spot hosts weekly Bingo nights, live music, and weddings and private events.

LAND MANAGER

Schiller Woods South
West Irving Park Road, East of Des Plaines River Road
Schiller Park, IL 60634
(800) 870-3666
www.fpdcc.com/places/locations/schiller-woods/

BREWERY/RESTAURANT

Short Fuse Brewing Company
5000 N. River Road
Schiller Park, IL 60176
(847) 260-5044
www.shortfusebrewing.com

Distance from trailhead: 1.4 mile

BLOOMINGDALE TRAIL

WALK AN ABANDONED TRAIN LINE TURNED TRAIL

NORTHWEST SIDE, WICKER PARK

▷··· STARTING POINT	···✗ DESTINATION
EAST TRAILHEAD IN WALSH PARK	**WEST TRAILHEAD**
🍺 BREWERY	🔲 HIKE TYPE
ORKENOY	**MODERATE**
🐾 DOG FRIENDLY	📅 SEASON
YES	**YEAR-ROUND**
$ FEES	🕐 DURATION
NO	**2 HOURS**
⛰ MAP REFERENCE	↦ LENGTH
CHICAGO PARK DISTRICT	**5.4 MILES** (ROUND-TRIP)
🔍 HIGHLIGHTS	〰 ELEVATION GAIN
CITY VIEWS, PUBLIC ART	**10 FEET**

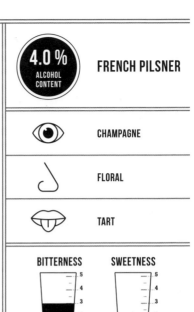

4.0%
ALCOHOL
CONTENT

FRENCH PILSNER

CHAMPAGNE

FLORAL

TART

BITTERNESS

5
4
3
2
1

SWEETNESS

5
4
3
2
1

HIKE DESCRIPTION

Stroll a defunct elevated rail line turned bike and walking trail through a vibrant, art-filled community green space. Hop off the line for a French-inspired pilsner at Nordic-inspired brewery and restaurant Orkenoy.

What was once an abandoned railroad line has been transformed into a tree-lined, art-filled 2.7-mile elevated bike and walking path—a much needed trailway for those on the Northwest Side that gives folks a safe path across the city from Wicker Park to Humboldt Park.

The Bloomingdale Trail project, which broke ground in August 2013 and was completed in June 2015, also included the addition of four new city parks as offshoots of the trail, which provide nice community green spaces, perfect for a quick picnic or some outdoor reading before hopping back on the trail.

For this hike, you'll start at the East Trailhead of the Bloomingdale Trail (also known as the 606 Trail), which is just off Ashland Avenue inside Walsh Park. The East Trailhead takes you up a long, windy ramp until you're up on the elevated path. Walkers should stay on the right and beware of bikers zooming by with their call, "On your left!"

One of the first things you'll notice is how green the trail is, especially for a concrete bike path. Although the path here is narrower than on its western stretch, it is still lined on both sides by gorgeous vegetation: large pine trees, thick green walls of trumpet vines with florescent pink flowers, and gorgeous bright red flowering sumacs are just some of the florae on show.

Another thing you'll notice? You're at eye level with the beautiful back-yard patios and rooftop gardens attached to the nearby Wicker Park condos, apartment buildings, and brownstones—a bonus for those of us who love to gaze at Chicago homes.

After just over three-quarters of a mile, you can hop off for a rest in the trail's first offshoot green space, Park 567, where you can climb around on some rocks or enjoy a quick rest. Then, you'll head further west and reach Kedzie Avenue in Logan Square, where the trail will widen and become more lush and a canopy will appear above you, finally offering some shady relief if it's a sunny day.

As you reach the Humboldt Park neighborhood, you'll see the colorful Kimball Arts Center building on your left, where you can stop at Orkenoy (unless you want to save it for the way back). Just past the arts center, you'll come to one of the trail's publicly displayed artworks: "Birds Watching" by Jenny Kendler, a 40-foot-long aluminum sculpture composed of a flock of 100 reflective birds' eyes of different sizes and colors. Just past the sculpture, you'll come to what is perhaps the prettiest stretch of the trail—a wide forest of quaking aspen trees, where you'll have the option to take a lovely offshoot dirt path through the forest.

Once you reach the westernmost point—the Ridgeway Trailhead—you'll wind your way up to a circular lookout point before heading back the way you came to reach the East trailhead at Ashland Avenue.

TURN-BY-TURN DIRECTIONS

1. From the East Trailhead in Walsh Park, head up the ramp to begin the hike.

2. At 0.5 miles, come to the Damen Art Plaza, where you can sit and look down on the city below.

3. At 0.8 miles, hop off at Park 567, a small green space. Then return to the main trail and continue straight.

4. At 1.8 miles, take a rest at some stadium seating with a view of Logan Park Boulevard.

5. At 2.0 miles, hop off at Julia de Burgos Park, a park with a large playground.

6. At 2.2 miles, you can take the Spaulding Avenue ramp down to our recommended brewery, Orkenoy (you can also choose to save the beer for the way back). Take the long ramp down and walk one block west to Orkenoy. Once you've enjoyed a brew, return to the trail.

7. At 2.3 miles, turn left on a small dirt path that leads through a wooded area and runs parallel to the bike path.

8. At 2.4 miles, as the dirt path ends, rejoin the bike path.

9. At 2.7 miles, at the West Trailhead, follow the circular path that winds around and up to a lookout point. Then head back down to start heading back east.

10. At 4.6 miles, if you're after another break, hop off at the busy Milwaukee Avenue exit to explore coffee shops, restaurants, bars, and shops.

11. At 5.4 miles, return to the East Trailhead in Walsh Park.

FIND THE TRAILHEAD

The East Trailhead is at 1806 North Ashland Avenue, inside Walsh Park. To get there from downtown Chicago, take I-90 W/I-94 W for about 4 miles, then take Exit 48A and bear right onto Armitage Avenue. Bear right again onto Ashland Avenue and head south for 0.2 miles. The trailhead inside Walsh Park will be on your right. Some streets in the Wicker Park neighborhood require permits to park, but parking is allowed on Ashland Avenue and some other nearby streets.

To get to the trailhead via public transportation from downtown Chicago, take the CTA Blue Line North and exit at the Division stop, at the corner of Division and Ashland. Walk North on Ashland for 0.7 miles, and the trailhead in Walsh Park will be on your left.

ORKENOY

Situated right on the 606 Trail, just off the Spaulding ramp and in a prime corner spot of the very cool and colorful Kimball Arts Center, the Nordic-inspired Orkenoy doesn't feel like your typical brewery and kitchen. The space is light and bright, full of pastel hues and tables with fun graphic prints. The menu isn't typical either: You'll find about half a dozen seasonal, rotating beers with descriptors more commonly found on a food menu, such as the Oyster Stout or Rhubarb and Dandelion Berliner Weiss. We recommend cooling down with a refreshing French Pilsner after a stroll on the sunny 606. It's a crisp, easy-drinking warm-weather beer that is more tart than hoppy and tastes more like sparkling wine than any pilsner has the right to.

You'll definitely want to come hungry, as Orkenoy's food is not your typical brewery fare. Think Nordic-inspired dishes such as the Short Rib Smorrebrod or Beet Pickled Eggs. Make sure to start with the caraway buns and Dijon mustard. Orkney also has a fun cocktail menu, wine list, and a small market where you can grab canned beer to go, as well as snacks, wine, and other artisanal treats. And don't forget to stroll through the halls of the arts center to check out some local art.

LAND MANAGER

Chicago Park District
1600-3750 W. Bloomingdale Avenue
Chicago, IL 60647
(312) 742-4622
www.the606.org

BREWERY/RESTAURANT

Orkenoy
1757 N. Kimball Avenue, Floor 1
Chicago, IL 60647
(312) 929-4024
www.Orkenoy.com

Distance from trailhead: 2.2 miles

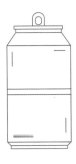

HUMBOLDT PARK NATURAL AREA

A NATURE WALK IN A BELOVED CITY PARK

WEST SIDE, HUMBOLDT PARK

▷··· STARTING POINT	···✗ DESTINATION
HUMBOLDT PARK BOATHOUSE	**NATURAL AREA**
☐ BREWERY	▦ HIKE TYPE
BUNGALOW BY MIDDLEBROW	**EASY**
● DOG FRIENDLY	▦ SEASON
YES	**YEAR-ROUND**
$ FEES	◷ DURATION
NO	**30 MINUTES**
⌂ MAP REFERENCE	↦ LENGTH
AT TRAILHEAD	**1.4 MILES** (LOOP)
◎ HIGHLIGHTS	∿ ELEVATION GAIN
LAGOON ISLAND, CITY VIEW	**13 FEET**

4.0 %
ALCOHOL CONTENT

BUNGALOW LAGER

BRIGHT GOLDEN YELLOW

FLORAL

CITRUS

BITTERNESS

SWEETNESS

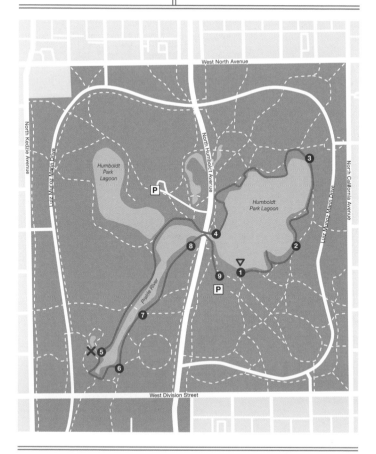

HIKE DESCRIPTION

 Stroll around a popular lagoon and wildlife area in the lively neighborhood of Humboldt Park. Then cool off with a refreshing lager at nearby Logan Square staple Bungalow by MiddleBrow.

The West Side neighborhood of Humboldt Park is the center of Puerto Rican culture in Chicago, named for the Humboldt (Alexander Von) Park, a gorgeous nearly 200-acre green space at its heart.

The park is home to a field house with a fitness center, soccer fields, tennis courts, and a smaller replica of the Chicago Cubs stadium known as "Little Cubs Field." But it's also home to arguably the most popular lagoon in Chicago. You can stroll around it or take in the views from the water by renting a giant swan-shaped paddle boat.

The lagoon itself made national news in 2019 when a 4-foot-long alligator—nicknamed Chance the Snapper—was found swimming in it. It took a seven-day operation to locate and rescue him. Locals came in droves to help search for the alligator and stayed to play music and celebrate the unlikely news story.

While the alligator and its search party are long gone, the park still has a celebratory feel to it. You can hear Puerto Rican music drifting up from nearby family gatherings, and the lagoon itself attracts locals to fish, bird watch, and hike. For this hike, you'll stroll around the lagoon and then head south along the prairie river to the natural area before looping back to where you start.

You'll begin near the historic Humboldt Park boathouse, which was designed in 1907 in the Prairie School architectural design. Take the path just east of the boathouse to begin the counterclockwise loop around the lagoon. The path alternates between a typical cement park path and a red gravel path that hugs the lagoon's edge.

Soon after you begin the hike, bear left and cross a bridge over to a charming island covered in tall wildflowers, including wild rye and white asters; enjoy a great view of the lagoon, then head back on the path.

After you loop around the lagoon (you'll get an impressive view of the Chicago skyline as you reach the western stretch), you'll head west along the beautiful prairie river, which is covered in lily pads. Continue along the path toward the natural area, where you can climb on rocks, take foot bridges over ponds, and enjoy being immersed in nature. The area is full of weeping willows and crabapple trees and the paths are lined by goldenrods.

If you're interested in a quick detour to the National Museum of Puerto Rican Arts & Culture, cross Division Street to reach the entrance. Even if there's no time to go inside, you can still check out the colorful murals in front of the Museum before returning to your hike that loops back around to the boathouse.

TURN-BY-TURN DIRECTIONS

1. Begin the trail on a cement path, marked by a large sign with a
    map and information, just east of the Humboldt Park boathouse.
    Just past the trailhead, bear left over a bridge to an island with a
    small loop trail, then return back to the path.

2. At 0.2 miles, bear left and then take another left to stay on the red
    gravel path that loops along the lagoon. Every so often, the red
    gravel path ends and turns back into a cement path. Continue
    following the counterclockwise loop.

3. At 0.3 miles, bear left and then take another left at the
    playground.

4. At 0.6 miles, stay straight to head underneath the North Humboldt
    Drive. overpass. Pass the Humboldt Park fieldhouse and then
    walk along the prairie river and through the natural area.

5. At 1.0 miles, take a sharp left to walk over large stone rocks, then
    take another left to loop around the South edge of the river. Turn
    left again and take a grey foot bridge over the wetland area.

6. At 1.1 miles, bear left at the fork.

7. At 1.2 miles, stay straight at the fork. Just past the fork, you'll see
    a stone path off to the left, which you can take down to a little
    wooden dock, which is perfect place to sit and read a book or
    have a picnic.

8. At 1.3 miles, continue straight to walk under the North Humboldt
    Drive overpass.

9. At 1.4 miles, arrive back at the boathouse.

FIND THE TRAILHEAD

To get to the boathouse from downtown Chicago, take I-290 West for
2.4 miles, then take Exit 27B toward California Avenue. Keep right and
merge onto Van Buren Street; continue for 0.4 miles, then bear right
onto Sacramento Boulevard and continue for 1.6 miles. At Augusta
Boulevard, just inside the park, Sacramento Boulevard turns into Humboldt Drive; continue for 0.5 miles. Shortly after you pass Division
Street, the entrance to the boathouse parking lot will be on your right.
To get to the park via public transportation from Downtown Chicago,
take the CTA Blue Line for about seven stops and exit at the Damen
stop. Walk north one block to North Avenue and take the No. 72 bus
west for ten stops, exiting at the Humboldt stop. Then walk south on
Humboldt Drive for about ten minutes, and the boathouse will be on
your left. The trailhead is just east of the Humboldt Park Boathouse, at
1301 North Humboldt Drive.

BUNGALOW BY MIDDLEBROW

The two things this Logan Square brewery, restaurant, and winery knows best? Beer and bread. When you first walk into this white, modern, sun-soaked space that feels much brighter and happier than your typical brewery, you're likely to be treated to the smell of delicious pizza and bread baking—and that's because the bakery is right in the middle of the brewery. You can watch the bakers hard at work—right beside the bartender pouring beer and wine and mixing cocktails. Bungalow has a fun, local feel, though it's so popular you'll likely want to make a reservation to avoid wait times. To accompany a pizza and a taste of their bread and housemade butter (you'll be thinking about the butter for days), we suggest ordering the self-titled Bungalow lager, a crisp and refreshing beer that makes for a perfect post-hike refreshment. Middlebrow refers to it as a "hyper-local lager," since it's brewed with grains from Sugar Creek Malt in Lebanon, IN. The name Bungalow is a reference to a style of small brick homes that have populated the city neighborhoods for decades. (In fact, there are more than 80,000 bungalow homes in Chicago's neighborhoods.) For non-beer drinkers, Middlebrow also recently launched Middlebrow Wine Co., Chicago's first natural wine company. Try a glass of their "Table Bread," made using grapes from southwest Michigan.

LAND MANAGER

Chicago Park District
4830 S. Western Avenue
Chicago, IL 60609
(312) 742-7529
www.chicagoparkdistrict.com/parks-facilities/humboldt-natural-area

BREWERY/RESTAURANT

Bungalow by Middle Brow
2840 W Armitage Ave.
Chicago, IL 60647
(773) 687-9076
www.middlebrowbeer.com

Distance from trailhead: 1.2 miles

CHICAGO RIVERWALK

WALK A PREVIOUSLY UNWALKABLE RIVER

DOWNTOWN, THE LOOP

▷⋯ STARTING POINT	⋯✕ DESTINATION
WEST ENTRANCE	**EAST ENTRANCE**
🍺 BREWERY	🀱 HIKE TYPE
CHICAGO BREWHOUSE RIVERWALK	**EASY** 🚶
🐾 DOG FRIENDLY	📅 SEASON
YES	**SPRING/SUMMER**
$ FEES	🕐 DURATION
NO	**50 MIN.**
🗺 MAP REFERENCE	⊢ LENGTH
AT TRAILHEAD	**3.2 MILES** (ROUND-TRIP)
🔍 HIGHLIGHTS	〰 ELEVATION GAIN
FLOATING GARDENS, BEER MUSEUM	**9 FEET**

CHICAGO RIVERWALK GOLDEN ALE

4.8 % ALCOHOL CONTENT

 LIGHT GOLD

 CITRUS

 SWEET, MALTY

BITTERNESS

SWEETNESS

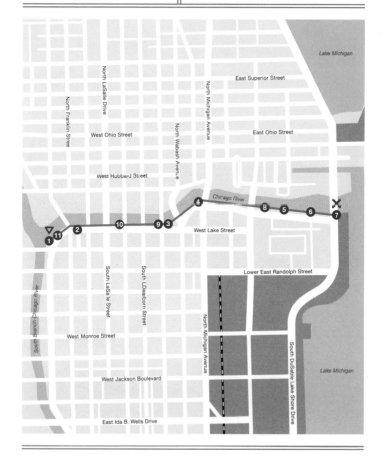

HIKE DESCRIPTION

See epic city views of Downtown Chicago as you walk the length of the iconic Chicago Riverwalk. Halfway along, stop at the Chicago Brewhouse that doubles as a beer museum and try its classic house ale, brewed by Revolution Brewing.

For a long time, architectural boat cruises, water taxis, and kayak tours were the only ways to travel along the Chicago River downtown. Then, in 2016, the Windy City built a modern gem in the Chicago Riverwalk—the perfect way to take in its history, architecture, art, and food scene.

The City and several architecture firms worked together to create a dazzling mix of gardens, spaces for waterfront restaurants, and cultural landmarks along a striking path with its own architectural accents and style. To see the entire Riverwalk, you'll stroll from the west end to the east end and back. If you can, do this walk during the warmer months—May through September—to take advantage of seasonal businesses. That said, if you prefer fewer crowds and aren't too bothered about stopping to taste the range of specialty Chicago dishes, a fall or winter stroll would still be lovely.

Starting at Lake Street, you'll first pass a colorful, welcoming mural of faces, part of an installation called "The People in Your Neighborhood" by Don't Fret, a local anonymous street muralist. You'll soon come to the greenest part of the walk, the Jetty—a beautiful floating wetland garden that sits in the middle of the river. The space is designed to provide a habitat for wildlife and is an interactive learning environment addressing the ecology of the river.

The Jetty is also a great place to catch a glimpse of the Chicago L Train as it roars above on the iconic Wells Street Bridge, a double-decker bascule bridge. As you walk underneath it, take time to appreciate the beautiful modern canopy of reflective stainless steel sheltering you. The steel is almost a work of art itself, beautifully reflecting the light from the water to the canopy and back onto the path.

Between each bridge, you'll find a stretch of new architectural treasures, the grandest of which is the River Theater between LaSalle and Clark Streets. The theater—a majestic, geometrical wonder designed by the famous architect Carol Ross Barney and her team—is a concrete ribbon of steps and walkways that begins at Wacker Drive and unfolds all the way down to the water, giving Chicagoans a space to sit, eat their lunch, and take in the river.

As you continue your walk past Wabash Avenue, you'll see the Chicago Brewhouse and stop for the recommended mid-walk pint—of course, you can also save it for when you're thirsty on the walk back (or stop both times). The restaurant and bar also houses an exhibition on the history of Chicago's craft beer scene.

The Vietnam Veterans Memorial by the State Street Bridge provides walkers a place to pause and reflect. From here, you'll continue toward the historic Magnificent Mile, a stretch of one-of-a-kind flagship retail stores, posh hotels, art, and restaurants. Just past Michigan Avenue, you can grab a ticket for an architecture boat cruise or rent a kayak and head out on the river yourself. The eastern part of the stretch is a little less crowded, but it's still peppered with lively outdoor restaurants and beer gardens, a playground, and more public art.

As you near the end of the Riverwalk, you'll pass through a long tunnel. Out the other side, you'll end the walk with views of the Navy Pier ferris wheel. The image makes a great photo op and is the perfect way to cap off an urban stroll that connects you to many important features of the city. From here, you'll turn and follow the same path back. There are also giant wooden lounge chairs near the end if you want to take a quick rest before heading back west.

TURN-BY-TURN DIRECTIONS

1. Begin the hike at the Riverwalk's west entrance at the junction of Wacker Drive and Lake Street.
2. At 0.2 miles, check out the floating river gardens called The Jetty and pass under the double-decker Wells Street Bridge.
3. At 0.7 miles, stop at the Vietnam Veterans Memorial and head into the Chicago Brewhouse Riverwalk for our recommended beer.
4. At 0.8 miles, pass under historic Michigan Avenue.
5. At 1.1 miles, stop and visit the US Navy Submarine Memorial. If you're with children, visit the riverside playground.
6. At 1.2 miles, stop to rent a kayak (if you feel like it).
7. At 1.3 miles, pass through a tunnel to reach the end of the Riverwalk. Stop for a quick glance at the Navy Pier ferris wheel before turning around and heading back the way you came.
8. At 1.5 miles (if hiking during the summer), stop for a snack or drink at one of several outdoor beer gardens.
9. At 2.0 miles, pass the historic corn cob towers near State Street.
10. At 2.3 miles, stop for a rest at the River Theater.
11. At 2.6 miles, finish the hike back where you started.

FIND THE TRAILHEAD

The west entrance to the Chicago Riverwalk is at the northwest corner of Wacker Drive and Lake Street. To get there by public transportation, take the CTA Brown, Blue, Green, Orange, Purple, or Pink Line train to the Clark and Lake stop, walk east three blocks, cross Wacker Drive and take a right. When you see the Riverwalk sign on your left take the stairs down to the trailhead. If you're taking the Metra train, exit at Ogilvie Transportation Center, walk three blocks north to Lake Street and take a right, then head east for two blocks and take a left onto Wacker Drive. The Riverwalk sign will be on your left.

CHICAGO BREWHOUSE/REVOLUTION BREWING

This seasonal taproom and restaurant is an ode to local brewing and boasts an impressive beer menu. Try the Chicago Riverwalk Golden Ale, brewed specifically for the taproom by Revolution Brewing, a stalwart brewery in Chicago. Revolution opened in 2010 and has grown to be the largest independent brewer in Illinois, producing dozens of beer styles. The ale is a crisp, drinkable summer beer that is reminiscent of a pilsner. Chicago Brewhouse doubles as a local beer museum where you can learn a plethora of facts like this one: 95% of Chicago beer is made with water from Lake Michigan and the Chicago River. If you're looking for a year-round place to get a good beer, hop off the Riverwalk at Michigan Avenue and head north to Crushed by Giants, 600 North Michigan Avenue. Order the Neon Werewolf IPA and snag a window seat for a beautiful view of downtown Chicago.

LAND MANAGER

City of Chicago
Department of Assets, Information and Services
2 North LaSalle Street, Floor 2
Chicago, IL 60602
(312) 744-3900
www.chicago.gov/city/en/sites/chicagoriverwalk/home.html

BREWERY/RESTAURANT

Chicago Brewhouse
31 East Riverwalk
Chicago, IL 60601
(312) 877-5766
www.chicagobrewhouse.com

Distance from trailhead: 0.6 miles

PALMISANO PARK

EXPERIENCE GREENSPACE INNOVATION ON THE SOUTH SIDE

SOUTH SIDE,
BRIDGEPORT

▷⋯ STARTING POINT	⋯✖ DESTINATION
TRAILHEAD SIGN AT HALSTED AND 27TH STREET	**TERRACED WETLANDS**
🍺 BREWERY	🌀 HIKE TYPE
DUNEYRR FERMENTA	**EASY**
🐾 DOG FRIENDLY	📅 SEASON
YES	**YEAR-ROUND**
$ FEES	🕐 DURATION
NO	**35 MINUTES**
🗺 MAP REFERENCE	↦ LENGTH
CHICAGO PARK DISTRICT	**1.4 MILES** (LOOP)
🔍 HIGHLIGHTS	〰 ELEVATION GAIN
ENTRY FOUNTAIN, CLIMBING ROCK	**125 FEET**

SAUVYN BLANC

ORANGE YELLOW

WHITE GRAPES,
PEACH

FRUITY,
WINE-FORWARD

BITTERNESS

SWEETNESS

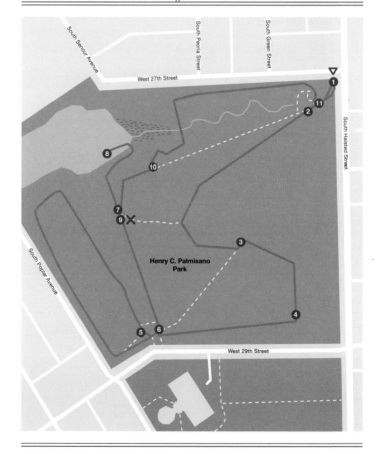

HIKE DESCRIPTION

Tour a one-time quarry and landfill that has been transformed into a charming sustainable wetlands and park. Then, sip the most innovative beer in Chicago at Duneyrr.

This hike begins at a typical Chicago Park District trailhead sign announcing the Henry C. Palmisano Nature Park. Soon after you enter the park, you'll spot a galvanized metal sculpture and water fountain known as the Entry Fountain. Take a moment here, as this sculpture sets the tone for what is anything but an ordinary walk in the park.

At the center of the fountain is an over 10-foot-tall metal sculpture of an old crane that stood in the park grounds back when it was a 26-acre quarry. Reclaimed water runs through a metal tube on the sculpture and drips down into a concrete runnel that carries it through terraced wetland cells and into a fishing pond, which you'll later tour. The water in the pond is recirculated underground and brought back to the fountain.

You'll next continue up a long walkway with an elevated view of the wetland area on your right. To your left is an open green hillside that's perfect for picnics and sunbathing. You'll continue along the walkway until you reach the top of the hill, where there's a great view of the Chicago skyline.

The hike continues down the hill past metal exercise equipment, inviting hikers to get their heart rate up with dips, chin-ups, and sit-ups. There's also a fun rock structure here; take this opportunity to express your inner Alex Honnold by free climbing the miniature 15-foot-tall mountain.

The climbing rock is part of a play area and a second community field with a looping jogging path. Walk the quick loop, meet back at the main path, and cross over a metal bridge to a fishing pond. At the pier, you'll see schools of fish, turtles, and ducks. It's a serene spot in the middle of a manufacturing-heavy area of Chicago.

As you come to the water's edge, you'll see tiered wetland cells on your right producing mini-waterfalls that cascade into the pond. It's a beautiful scene, especially considering that, from the late 1830s until 1970, this was a limestone quarry.

Approximately 400 million years before the Illinois Stone and Lime Company began quarry operations, this area formed part of an ancient coral reef (fossils found here are on display at the Field Museum of Natural History). As you continue on the path past the pond, an elevated metal bridge system takes you through the wetland cells for a closer look at these earthen basins and their lush aquatic plant-life before you loop back to the Entry Fountain. This short but sweet hike is a great way to appreciate a rejuvenated community park on the industrial south side.

TURN-BY-TURN DIRECTIONS

1. As you begin the hike, stop for a look at the Entry Fountain statue before continuing on the same path.
2. At the fork just past the statue, bear left on the path to go up the hill.
3. At 0.2 miles, at the highest point of the hike, take in views of the city and then take the second right.
4. At 0.3 miles, bear right to continue the loop trail.
5. At 0.5 miles, stay straight at the fork to head up stone steps and then bear right onto a smaller gravel path to start the second, smaller loop.
6. At 0.8 miles, complete the smaller loop and stop to climb on the rock structure; then bear left to continue on the main loop trail.
7. At 0.9 miles, head straight for a view of the pond.
8. At 1.0 miles, come to the edge of the metal pier and then turn around and head back to the main loop.
9. At 1.1 miles, make a hard left to follow the loop and head up an elevated metal bridge for a view of the terraced wetlands.
10. At 1.2 miles, bear left, and then another left, and then bear right onto a concrete path.
11. At 1.4 miles, return to the Entry Fountain and bear left to reach the trailhead.

FIND THE TRAILHEAD

The trailhead is located in the northeast end of the park, at the corner of Halsted Street and 27th Street. Via public transportation, take the CTA Orange Line train to the Halsted stop. From there, walk 0.3 miles down Archer Avenue and turn right onto Halsted Avenue; the park is just past the turn. Alternatively, take the Blue Line train to the Halsted Avenue and 26th Street stop and then head south on Halsted for 175 feet to get to the trailhead. You can also take the No. 62 Harlem bus and exit at the Archer and Lowe stop. Take Archer Avenue for less than 0.5 miles and turn right on Halsted. Drivers can avail of free street parking on Halsted Avenue.

DUNEYRR FERMENTA

A modern hike deserves a modern beer, and Duneyrr Fermenta delivers just that with its intensely flavored brews that have been fermented with wine. The brewery launched in 2021 and instantly made waves locally. It's the brainchild of Tyler Davis, a brewer who trained at the Siebel Institute of Technology in Chicago, and draws in crowds with its beer-wine hybrids and mixed-culture beers. The beers make for an explosive, flavorful tasting experience. Standouts include an IPA of mosaic and galaxy hops mixed with Pinot Gris grapes and a wild session ale co-fermented with orange wine. Sauvyn Blanc, a vineyard ale co-fermented with Sauvignon Blanc grapes and passion fruit, one of the brewery's flagship beers, has a beautifully dry, yet bright and tropical flavor and is a must-try.

Duneyrr Fermenta is also home to partner brewery Moderne Dunne, which produces more classic-style beers like pilsners and porters with anything but classic flavors. The beers incorporate experimental hops and are out-of-this-world smooth. Combined, the breweries are the beer world's answer to fine dining. The elegance of the small taproom's beers is also reflected in its décor and exceptional cheeseboards. The name Duneyrr means "winds of change" in Norse mythology, and this innovative brewery exudes just that.

LAND MANAGER

McGuane Park
2700 South Halsted Street
Chicago, IL 60608
(312) 747-6497
www.chicagoparkdistrict.com/parks-facilities/palmisano-henry-park

BREWERY/RESTAURANT

Duneyrr Fermenta
2337 South Michigan Avenue
Chicago, IL 60616
(312) 374-1903
www.duneyrr.com

Distance from trailhead: 1.6 miles

MCKINLEY PARK NATURAL AREA

CIRCLE A RARE LAGOON IN A HISTORIC COMMUNITY SPACE

SOUTHWEST SIDE, MCKINLEY PARK

▷··· STARTING POINT	···✕ DESTINATION
ENTRANCE AT 37TH ST. AND DAMEN AVE.	**WILLIAM MCKINLEY STATUE**
🍺 BREWERY	🁢 HIKE TYPE
MARZ COMMUNITY BREWING CO.	**EASY**
🐾 DOG FRIENDLY	📅 SEASON
YES	**YEAR-ROUND**
$ FEES	🕐 DURATION
NO	**40 MINUTES**
⛰ MAP REFERENCE	↦ LENGTH
AT TRAILHEAD	**1.5 MILES** (LOOP)
🔎 HIGHLIGHTS	〰 ELEVATION GAIN
LAGOON, MCKINLEY STATUE	**9 FEET**

5.5 %
ALCOHOL
CONTENT

JUNGLE BOOGIE
PALE WHEAT ALE

DARK CARAMEL

SUBTLE TEA

**MALTY,
DRY FRUIT**

BITTERNESS   SWEETNESS

HIKE DESCRIPTION

Stroll around a peaceful lagoon and explore a large park that has been a vital community hub since 1901. Then head to Marz Community Brewing for more good company and a pint of the vibrant Jungle Boogie.

McKinley (William) Park comprises nearly 72 acres of vital community space in a region of Chicago that is mostly devoid of greenery. Thriving city life stretches out for miles in every direction from the park's perimeter, and McKinley acts as a community hub, connecting the many surrounding neighborhoods. It caters to every activity and includes a swimming pool, seasonal skating rink, tennis courts, two gyms, outdoor basketball courts, baseball fields, and soccer fields. For outdoor enthusiasts, the park offers a lagoon to fish in and a series of short nature paths. While the lagoon pales in size compared to the Humboldt Park Lagoon, it offers walkers a peaceful place to stroll and has a rich history.

The park was established in October 1901 in what was formerly an underdeveloped space and was named in honor of William McKinley, the 25th President of the United States who was assassinated in September 1901. More than a year later, it opened to the public. This historic park was the first public green space in the crowded tenement neighborhoods near the center of Chicago. It was so widely used that it inspired the opening of more parks a few years later in other neighborhoods on the south side.

The community idyll is still alive and well in McKinley Park. You'll experience it firsthand on this hike, which, though hardly taxing, offers an inspiring opportunity to see large numbers of people gathered in this

shared space. Every inch of the park serves a purpose, and you'll gain insight into the park's thoughtful planning and design as you tour its grounds.

On our hike, we'll avoid the larger fieldhouse and communal areas and instead start at the trailhead near the lagoon. A sign points you down a skinny gravel path along a fence, and you'll follow it through tall prairie grass and a designated nature area. The trail then leads you to several wood-chip paths funneling toward a slightly elevated natural area with tree stumps and a pretty overlook of the lagoon.

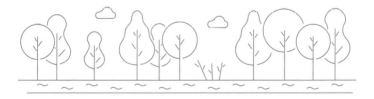

You'll follow one of the wood-chip trails until it meets a paved path that leads to the lagoon. The small lagoon is full of swans and other birds, so take your time to stop and admire them before heading away from the water on a paved path that circles the park grounds. Here's where you'll see families picnicking, soccer teams at play on turf, youth baseball games, pickup basketball, and all sorts of people gathered to enjoy each other's company. You'll also come upon a statue of William McKinley overlooking the park named in his honor.

This small circuit joins back up to the lagoon-side path exactly where you left it to round off this brief but charming hike.

TURN-BY-TURN DIRECTIONS

1.   Set off from the trailhead on the small gravel path that hugs the vast edge of the park.
2.   At. 0.2 miles, bear right onto a wood-chip path.
3.   At 0.3 miles, bear right to stay on the wood-chip path and curve toward the lagoon.
4.   At 0.4 miles, bear right to stay on the limestone path along the lagoon.
5.   At 0.5 miles, bear left on a concrete path and then take a quick right to loop around the sports fields.
6.   At 0.6 miles, bear left at the fork.
7.   At 0.7 miles, bear right to stay on the loop trail.
8.   At 0.8 miles, take a right—check out a softball, soccer, or tennis match.
9.   At 0.9 miles, reach the statue of William McKinley, the 25th President of the United States.
10. At 1.1 miles, bear right.
11. At 1.1 miles, bear left to get back on the limestone lagoon path.
12. At 1.3 miles, bear right to go over a boardwalk, then take another right to continue on the path.
13. At 1.5 miles, arrive at the trailhead to finish the hike.

FIND THE TRAILHEAD

The McKinley Park entrance is at the corner of West 37th Street and South Damen Avenue in the McKinley Park neighborhood of Chicago. It is accessible on the CTA 49 Western Bus. Get off at the stop at Western Avenue and Pershing Road, walk east to South Damen Avenue, and then turn left and walk to the corner of West 37th Street to find the trailhead.

MARZ COMMUNITY BREWING CO.

Arguably the hippest brewery in Chicago, Marz makes for an incredibly fun stop after the warm community vibes of McKinley Park. The hike pairs nicely with a Jungle Boogie, a vibrant pale wheat ale made with Rooibos tea. Like the brewery itself, the beer has a unique flavor. Dry hops, sweet stone-fruit flavors, and tea blend to anchor a beer with incredible character. Marz also crafts temporary offshoots of the staple, such as a Jungle Boogie with blueberry and one with pear.

The Iron Street taproom is a joy to visit—a lively neon-lit warehouse location with an eclectic interior design. The space has cheeky modern art everywhere and exudes cool (it has an arcade and vending machines selling old magazines, kitschy toys, and snacks). The brewery is owned by the Marszewski family, a pair of brothers and their mother who have had a tremendous impact on the South Side. Ed is the president of Marz Brewing, and his brother Mike owns Maria's Packaged Goods, a renowned bar originally owned by their mother that serves Polish- and Korean-inspired foods to honor their parents. Their mother, Maria, is often referred to as the "Duchess de Bridgeport," the South Side neighborhood where the family resides and operates Maria's. Like Ed, she is a huge supporter of the arts. Ed has opened a second Marz taproom on the North Side and continues philanthropic efforts in the City.

LAND MANAGER

McKinley Park
2210 West Pershing Road
Chicago, IL 60609
(312) 747-6527
www.chicagoparkdistrict.com/parks-facilities/mckinley-william-park

BREWERY/RESTAURANT

Marz Community Brewing Co.
The Iron Street Taproom
3630 South Iron Street
Chicago, IL 60609
(773) 579-1935
www.marz.beer

Distance from trailhead: 1 mile

WASHINGTON PARK
NATURAL AREA

SEE A SLICE OF NATURE BETWEEN MUSEUMS

SOUTH SIDE,
WOODLAWN

▷⋯ STARTING POINT	⋯✗ DESTINATION
PAYNE DRIVE AND 57TH STREET	TIP OF BYNUM ISLAND
🍺 BREWERY	🗺 HIKE TYPE
WHINER BEER COMPANY	EASY
🐾 DOG FRIENDLY	📅 SEASON
YES	YEAR-ROUND
$ FEES	🕐 DURATION
NO	50 MINUTES
⛰ MAP REFERENCE	↦ LENGTH
CHICAGO PARK DISTRICT	1.9 MILES (LOOP)
🔎 HIGHLIGHTS	〰 ELEVATION GAIN
FOUNTAIN OF TIME STATUE	4 FEET

LE TUB WILD FARMHOUSE ALE

6.4 % ALCOHOL CONTENT

 CLOUDY GOLD

 CLOVER, LEMON PEEL

 LEMON, WHITE GRAPE

BITTERNESS

SWEETNESS

HIKE DESCRIPTION

Visit a unique nature area and the Father of Time. End the hike with a Le Tub at Whiner Beer Company.

Washington Park almost feels as if it was dropped into the city, in the midst of roadways, museums, the University of Chicago, and the lakefront. Chicagoans are thankful for it, of course, but the park is definitely in a high-traffic zone. Directly across one street is the DuSable Black History Museum, while a block or two away are the heralded Museum of Science and Industry and other art museums and schools. This bustling area bleeds into the park, which itself houses a work of art but also maintains its own quiet calm.

The ideal spot to start exploring the park from is across the street from the DuSable Museum, on a path that begins just east of Payne Drive and 57th Street.

Beginning here in springtime, you'll be greeted by the smell of lilacs as you walk through tall prairie grass and take in views of Washington Lagoon. You'll veer left onto a trail that circles the lagoon, which is flanked by tall fescue and Kentucky bluegrass.

As you walk the lagoon, you'll soon spot an impressive, courtly sculpture on your left. Exit the path to view the Fountain of Time statue, created in 1922 by the prominent Chicago sculptor Lorado Taft. The sculpture is a beautiful but grim presence, a stone representation of Father Time presiding over a wave of human figures and a pool.

After merging back onto the path, you'll cross a quaint fishing bridge. Keep an eye out for herons and cranes as you continue to circle the lagoon. You'll soon reach a stunning tree-lined street reminiscent of Central Park. Extend the loop to walk under the canopy of trees and then return toward where you started. From there, you'll take a hidden path toward Bynum Island and encounter a whole new aspect of the park.

On either side of this path there are offshoot paths under trees that lead you to resting spots along the water. Gorgeous cattails, aster, and sumac abound, bringing an exotic feel to the island. The walk leads to an activity area run by the Chicago Park District in which kids can experience overnight camping and activities like wall climbing. Washington Park expanded in the 1930s to serve the park district and the growing African American population around it. It now boasts an aquatic center, sports fields, and this unique activity area.

TURN-BY-TURN DIRECTIONS

1. Begin the hike at the bird sanctuary sign by a small waterfall.
2. At 0.1 miles, bear left to join the main paved path that takes you around the Loop.
3. At 0.3 miles, visit the Fountain of Time statue; then continue along the Loop.
4. At 0.4 miles, back on the main Loop, take a footbridge over a fishing pier and continue along the south end of the lagoon.
5. At 0.6 miles, go straight at the fork.
6. At 0.8 miles, stay left at the fork. Pass a garden turnabout and continue straight down the tree-lined path. Go straight at the next garden turnabout.
7. At 1.4 miles, at 57th Street, bear right; then take another right by the restrooms onto a gravel path to head out onto the island.
8. At 1.5 miles, stay straight at the fork.
9. At 1.6 miles, stay straight at the fork to remain on the gravel path and head over the bridge.
10. At 1.7 miles, once over the bridge, bear right and make a small loop before heading back to the bridge and taking the trail back the way you came, leaving the island.
11. At 1.9 miles, bear right to go up the stone steps to return to the trailhead.

FIND THE TRAILHEAD

The trailhead is at a bird sanctuary sign near a small waterfall and public restrooms (which are often closed), just east of the intersection of Payne Drive and 57th Street. From the city center, head south on South Lake Shore Drive/US Highway 41 for 3 miles, take the Oakwood Boulevard exit, and bear right onto East Oakwood Boulevard. Take a quick left onto South Cottage Grove Avenue and continue for 2 miles; then bear right onto 57th Street and head one block west to Payne Drive. Turn left on Payne Drive; you should be able to find parking here.

Via public transportation, take the CTA Red Line train to the Garfield stop; then walk south for three minutes to the Garfield Red Line Station bus stop. Take the 55 bus east for 8 stops, exiting at the Morgan and Russell Drive stop inside Washington Park. Head south for 0.3 miles to the trailhead.

WHINER BEER COMPANY

Located inside an innovative facility called The Plant, Whiner Beer Company is stunning. Rows of community tables have living plants built into the middle of them; you'll also find beautiful exposed brick, pool tables, Bingo games, and great beer. The flagship brew, Le Tub, is one of the best wild styles in the city, a barrel-aged, wild saison that bursts with tartness but has strong Belgian notes on the back end. The can has a witty French-like cartoon drawing of a man in a bathtub, bathing in beer while a cat watches. The name Le Tub honors the brewery's French influence and barrel-aging process.

Whiner produces three different variants of Le Tub: a watermelon version, a blueberry variant, and a lime, cucumber, and salt adaptation. All of the beers are dry-hopped with dry fruit flavors. The operation is the brainchild of Brian Taylor and Ria Neri, who studied at the Siebel Institute. Taylor, the brewmaster, has worked at Chicago's Goose Island, Flying Dog in Denver, and Boulevard Brewing in Kansas City.

LAND MANAGER

Washington (George) Park
5531 South King Drive
Chicago, IL 60615
(773) 256-1248
www.chicagoparkdistrict.com/parks-facilities/washington-george-park

BREWERY/RESTAURANT

Whiner Beer Company
1400 West 46th Street
Chicago, IL 60609
(773) 475-6189
www.whinerbeer.com

Distance from trailhead: 3.5 miles

CHICAGO SUBURBS

FORT SHERIDAN

STROLL AROUND A FORMER ARMY BASE WITH LAKE VIEWS

NORTH SHORE,
LAKE FOREST, IL

▷⋯ STARTING POINT	⋯✕ DESTINATION
FORT SHERIDAN BEACH PARKING LOT	**FORT SHERIDAN NATIONAL CEMETERY**
🍺 BREWERY	🔀 HIKE TYPE
BROKEN TEE BREWING CO.	**EASY** 🚶
🐾 DOG FRIENDLY	📅 SEASON
YES	**YEAR-ROUND**
$ FEES	🕐 DURATION
NO	**45 MINUTES**
⛰ MAP REFERENCE	↦ LENGTH
FOREST PRESERVES OF LAKE COUNTY	**1.9 MILES** (LOOP)
🔍 HIGHLIGHTS	〰 ELEVATION GAIN
MILITARY CEMETERY, PRAIRIE VIEWS	**160 FEET**

5.2 %
ALCOHOL CONTENT

BEERANTONI ITALIAN PILSNER

	WHITE GOLD
	RIND, CITRUS
	CRISP LEMON

BITTERNESS	SWEETNESS

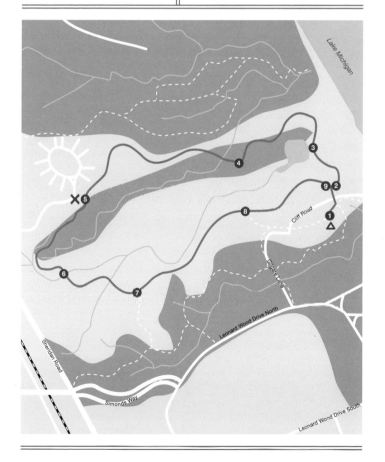

HIKE DESCRIPTION

Honor war heroes on this relaxing hike across historical military grounds before retreating to Broken Tee Brewing to sip an Italian-style pilsner.

Fort Sheridan and its vast prairie campus became an operational US Army training ground in 1889 and stayed active until 1993. It is now home to one of the few free beaches along Lake Michigan, with a beautiful 70-foot bluff overlooking the lake and nearly 4 miles of trails.

Designed for birdwatchers, the Birding Trail Loop offers a chance to spot more than 230 species of birds known to fly the area and is a relaxing way to take in the beauty of the prairie grass and views of Lake Michigan while honoring the former military presence in the area.

An old artillery station—now used as a post for birdwatching—sits along the walk, as does the Fort Sheridan National Cemetery, which invites hikers in to view the uniform rows of white gravestones dating back to 1890. The cemetery is also home to a monument dedicated to Chaplain Major Edward Vattman, who is buried there and served as a Chaplain during World War I. At the end of the hike, a paved trail guides you to the beach to enjoy a swim and cooldown—and to see a historic tank.

As for the Birding Loop Trail, a wide paved path kicks things off just outside the parking lot, where a large bright sign announces the trailhead. Lake Michigan sits majestically to your right, sending blustery winds over the low prairie grass. The paved path soon turns and gives way to a 10-foot-wide grass path that you'll follow for the rest of the hike. This mowed grass path cuts through what feels like endless prairie, where military service members once performed training exercises and lived in tents learning to endure wintry conditions.

The history of the path gives the walk a weighty significance. You'll stroll along through tall, waving grasses to the sounds of singing birds. The trail curls, and you'll soon find yourself walking over a striking iron bridge that crosses above a 20-foot-deep ravine, and then over another beautiful wooden bridge. This serene, just under two-mile walk over rolling terrain passes under large oak trees and cuts through savanna grass with a range of flowering plants and milkweed.

To extend your hike, you can walk the sandy shore of Lake Michigan for another three-quarters of a mile.

TURN-BY-TURN DIRECTIONS

1. Begin the hike at the large trail map in the beach parking lot and take an almost immediate left at the sign for the Birding Trail Loop.
2. At 0.1 miles, bear right on a paved trail at the fork.
3. At 0.2 miles, head straight at the sign to follow the Birding Trail Loop onto a grass path.
4. At 0.5 miles, cross the iron bridge over the ravine.
5. At 0.9 miles, stop by the Fort Sheridan National Cemetery.
6. At 1.2 miles, cross the wooden bridge.
7. At 1.4 miles, continue straight at the Birding Trail Loop sign.
8. At 1.6 miles, continue straight at the Birding Trail Loop sign.
9. At 1.9 miles, bear right and then take another quick right to arrive back at the trailhead in the parking lot.

FIND THE TRAILHEAD

To find the Birding Trail Loop, head to the parking lot for Fort Sheridan Beach. From Chicago, take IL 90 West and IL 94 West—the highways merge—and continue on IL 94 West for 21 miles. Stay left to merge onto 94 West toward US 41 North; follow this for just over 6 miles before turning onto Old Elm Road and then onto Cliff Road, which takes you to the beach parking lot.

BROKEN TEE BREWING CO.

With its modest, golf-themed decor, Broken Tee Brewery fits easily into the affluent North Shore area, which is home to a number of popular golf courses. That said, the brewery's name isn't a nod to the courses nearby but rather to the fact that the owner, Paul Bumbaco, spent two decades as a golf professional at golf clubs. This small brewery, which has humble, homebrewing origins, has only been open a few short years but has already earned a reputation for producing wonderful beer. All the beers have golf-themed names, such as Bogey Train, Power Fade, and Swing Hard, except one: Bierantoni pays homage to the brewery's location. The brewery took over a restaurant run by Al and Jane Pierantoni that served diners faithfully for 55 years.

Bierantoni is a smooth, easy-drinking Italian pilsner and the perfect way to toast the Fort Sheridan walk. The beer is golden, dry, and flavorful with lemony notes. There aren't many beers on tap at the brewery, but it does offer a unique coffee lager and a hard seltzer and boasts a tasty menu of American bar food, including a hot fried chicken sandwich, a smash burger, and a cheesesteak, along with fries, curds, and appetizers. The taproom sits in a quaint downtown area of Highwood, Illinois, right beside the Metra railway that serves Chicago and the suburbs.

LAND MANAGER

Forest Preserves of Lake County
117 Sheridan Road
Lake Forest, IL 60045
(800) 870-3666
www.lcfpd.org/fort-sheridan

BREWERY/RESTAURANT

BROKEN TEE BREWING CO.
406 Green Bay Road
Highwood, IL 60040
(847) 780-3043
www.brokenteebrewco.com

Distance from trailhead: 2 miles

SKOKIE LAGOONS

A WET AND WILD ISLAND TRAIL

NORTH SHORE,
SKOKIE, IL

▷··· STARTING POINT	···✘ DESTINATION
FOREST WAY GROVE PARKING LOT	**NIKE ISLAND**
🍺 BREWERY	HIKE TYPE
RAVINIA BREWING CO.	**MODERATE**
🐾 DOG FRIENDLY	SEASON
YES	**YEAR-ROUND**
$ FEES	⏲ DURATION
NO	**1 HOUR 30 MIN.**
⌂ MAP REFERENCE	↦ LENGTH
FOREST PRESERVES OF COOK COUNTY	**3.5 MILES** (LOLLIPOP LOOP)
🔎 HIGHLIGHTS	〰 ELEVATION GAIN
A TUNNEL-LIKE STRETCH OF FOREST	**55 FEET**

DIVERSEY STATION PALE ALE

CLOUDY YELLOW

LEMON, PINE

TROPICAL, ZESTY

BITTERNESS   SWEETNESS

HIKE DESCRIPTION

Visit the jungle of Nike Island, where you'll get dirty kicking along a rugged lagoon trail; then dock at Ravinia Brewing for a juicy Diversey Station session ale.

The just-under-900-acre Skokie Lagoons is a rare landscape of connected waterways in the Chicago area that visitors frequently explore in rented kayaks and canoes. And while this popular outdoor destination is known for water-based activities, including fishing, it also boasts many great hiking trails on its shorelines and islands.

Skokie Lagoons was originally the homeland of the Ojibwa, Ottawa, and Potawatomi Native American tribes, who knew the area as an incredibly large marshland. Europeans began settling in the region in the early 1800s, and in the 1930s the wetland was transformed into the artificially constructed lagoons, channels, and islands that visitors still see today. The plans to create a recreational lagoon space came as part of Franklin D. Roosevelt's Civilian Conservation Corps project to put unemployed laborers to work during the Great Depression.

When hiking in this popular wetland and prairie grass habitat, the best trail is perhaps the one less traveled—the Skokie Lagoons Inner Trail, also known to locals as Nike Island. Don't let the name fool you, however: leave your Nikes behind and lace up your boots, because this hike is bumpy and likely to be muddy.

The Inner Lagoon Trail is not marked by any signs along the way—not even at the trailhead. It's a deep-woods walk and you just have to have faith that the old path will circle you back.

96

You'll start this hike on a wide gravel access road that narrows as it bends around the lagoon and disappears into the woods. To find it, first look for the park's Forest Way Grove entrance. The park has three entrances, with clear signs directing you toward each one. Once on Forest Way Drive, you'll head for the large lagoon. Before you reach its banks, you'll come to a gravel parking area on the side of the road. From there, you'll be able to see the wide gravel trail where your hike begins.

As soon as you head off, you'll be treated to beautiful views of the water—until the trail narrows and guides you into dense forest, that is. Early on, you'll reach an opening in the trees and see that there is water on either side of you—a cool reminder that you're on an island trail. The rocky path soon heads back into heavy forest, and the hike gets ever more delightful as the path continues to narrow and your surroundings get wilder.

As the trail makes its way around the island, you'll find yourself crowded by low-hanging boughs and four-foot-tall grass (if you're hiking in the summer or early fall).

The walk is usually a relatively isolated adventure, and while the route might sound difficult to follow due to being unmarked, the path guides you well; when in doubt, you can follow the water's edge. Disclaimer: if it has been raining, expect mud, and potentially some hidden segments of trail.

TURN-BY-TURN DIRECTIONS

1. From the north end of the Forest Way Grove parking area, follow the unmarked wide gravel path (not the paved bike path).
2. At 0.2 miles, bear left at the fork to explore Nike Island.
3. At 0.7 miles, come to a small clearing and bear right at the fork.
4. At 1.0 miles, at the top of a small hill, bear left to begin the loop trail around the island.
5. At 1.7 miles, arrive at the most southernmost point of the island and continue the loop.
6. At 2.5 miles, arrive back at the top of the small hill to complete the loop. Bear left to head down the hill.
7. At 2.8 miles, come to a small clearing and bear left at the fork.
8. At 3.3 miles, bear right to leave the island and head back to the trailhead.
9. At 3.5 miles, return to the trailhead and the parking area.

FIND THE TRAILHEAD

From Chicago, follow IL-94 West for around 20 miles and then take the Willow Road Exit. Once on Willow Road, drive for about half a mile and then take a left onto North Forest Way. Continue on this road for a little over a mile before arriving at the gravel parking area of the Forest Way Grove entrance to Skokie Lagoons. The unmarked trailhead is at the north end of the parking area—this is the only way to access the Inner Trail.

RAVINIA BREWING CO.

Named for the Ravinia neighborhood in Highland Park, Illinois, Ravinia Brewing opened its doors in 2016 and has since operated an outdoor patio–driven brewery in the business district of the suburb. The neighborhood is also home to the Ravinia Festival, a long-running outdoor music venue that is the hallmark of the area. (In fact, the founding brewers needed to stall the launch of their company because the venue's owners objected to their use of the Ravinia name. The brewers were able to satisfy the owners by enlarging the font of the words "Brewing Company" on the cans.)

Ravinia Brewing later opened a Logan Square–based taproom in the City; both its establishments offer Mexican food, and their tacos are a particular highlight. They've also created one of the more flavorful pale ales around: The Diversey Station, a "juicy session pale ale," is a mainstay. It's a very easy-drinking pale ale that perfectly complements this not-so-easy hike. The tropical flavors also match the hike's jungle feel. The beer won a bronze award in the 2022 Great American Beer Festival for best Hazy American Pale Ale. Diversey Station is a nod to the Logan Square neighborhood, and the can showcases a slick drawing of a significant monument and movie theater in the neighborhood.

LAND MANAGER

Forest Preserves of Cook County
536 North Harlem Avenue
River Forest, IL 60305
(800) 870-3666
www.fpdcc.com/places/locations/skokie-lagoons

BREWERY/RESTAURANT

Ravinia Brewing Co.
582 Roger Williams Avenue
Highland Park, IL 60035
(847) 780-8127
www.raviniabrewingcompany.com

Distance from trailhead: 3 miles

THE GROVE

STROLL THROUGH A HISTORIC OAK-HICKORY SAVANNA

NORTH SHORE
GLENVIEW

▷⋯ STARTING POINT	⋯✕ DESTINATION
THE INTERPRETIVE CENTER	**NATIVE AMERICAN VILLAGE**
🍺 BREWERY	🏷 HIKE TYPE
MACUSHLA BREWING CO.	**EASY** 🚶
🐾 DOG FRIENDLY	📅 SEASON
NO	**YEAR-ROUND**
$ FEES	🕐 DURATION
NO	**45 MINUTES**
🗺 MAP REFERENCE	↦ LENGTH
GLENVIEW PARK DISTRICT	**1.7 MILES** (LOLLIPOP LOOP)
🔍 HIGHLIGHTS	〰 ELEVATION GAIN
WILDLIFE SIGHTINGS, EDUCATIONAL HISTORY	**1 FOOT**

6.6%
ALCOHOL
CONTENT

HOLLA-PENO IPA

 GOLD

 CITRUS,
PEPPER

 JALAPENO PEPPER,
ORANGE

BITTERNESS   SWEETNESS

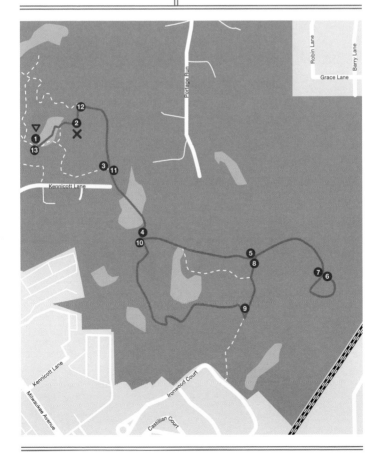

HIKE DESCRIPTION

Take an educational tour of a beautiful oak-hickory savanna at the former home of a family of famed local horticulturalists. Then stop by a local woman-owned brewery for a delicious Jalapeno IPA.

An ideal lunchtime stroll or nature walk, the Grove is a unique ecological site and national landmark filled with history and wildlife.

The Grove is the former home of visionary horticulturist and educator Dr. John Kennicott, who came to the area from New Orleans with his family in 1836. He developed the Grove into the first major nursery in Northern Illinois. His son, Robert Kennicott, became a prominent naturalist and founded the Chicago Academy of Sciences, which is now known as the Peggy Notebaert Nature Museum in Chicago.

You can wander the grounds and see the exterior of the former Kennicott home, a majestic Gothic Revival house built in 1856.

For this nature walk, though, after you park in the East Parking Lot, follow signs to the Grove's magnificent log-cabin Interpretive Center.

You'll begin by taking a boardwalk over a small wetland pool, where you'll spot bright green frogs in the summer months. Then, head to a gravel trail to stroll amongst the oak and hickory trees.

As a tribute to the Kennicotts, who were devoted to education, the volunteers at the Grove have included points along the trails to educate nature enthusiasts on important parts of the land's history, making the

Grove feel like an outdoor museum. Shortly after you begin this hike, you'll come to the Native American Village, where you can explore a bark longhouse and tipi—replicas of Potawatomi dwellings that were once on this property.

Back on the trail, the Grove savanna provides the most intense auditory experience of all the hikes in this book. A chorus of bird calls from blue jays and woodpeckers fills the air, and chipmunks scamper among the fallen trees. It's a true forest hike, with tree coverage and tall weeds that are perfect for grazing deer. (We saw nearly half a dozen.)

For such a short hike, there are a lot of forks in the road. Follow the signs with the green hiker icon. At 0.7 miles, you'll come to a lollipop-style trail that is tacked onto the main loop. It provides a deeper reach into a beautiful stretch of woods with more wetland ponds.

Back on the main trail, you'll continue your loop and arrive back at the Interpretive Center, where you can see snakes (this time behind glass) and giant snapping turtles in a habitat. You'll also learn about the history of the Kennicotts. It's beautifully designed, much like the Grove itself.

TURN-BY-TURN DIRECTIONS

1. Begin your hike in front of the Interpretive Center by taking the boardwalk over the pond. When the boardwalk ends, bear left onto the gravel trail.
2. At 0.1 miles, visit the Native American Village; then return to the trail and take a right at the fork.
3. At 0.2 miles, stay straight at the fork and take the boardwalk over the wetland pond.
4. At 0.3 miles, bear left to begin the lollipop-style trail.
5. At 0.5 miles, bear left to begin a second lollipop-style trail.
6. At 0.7 miles, bear left at the fork to loop around the top of the lollipop trail.
7. At 0.8 miles, return to the fork and bear left.
8. At 1.0 miles, complete the lollipop trail and bear left to return to the main loop. Just ahead, bear left at the fork to stay on the main loop.
9. At 1.2 miles, bear right to continue the loop.
10. At 1.4 miles, complete the main loop and cross back over the boardwalk.
11. At 1.5 miles, stay straight at the fork.
12. At 1.6 miles, bear right to walk over the boardwalk.
13. At 1.7 miles, return to the Interpretive Center.

FIND THE TRAILHEAD

The trailhead for this hike is at the Interpretive Center, which is a short walk east of the East Parking Lot. To get to the Grove from Chicago, take I-94 North to Exit 37A and then Dempster Avenue west for 3.3 miles. Then bear right on Milwaukee Avenue and continue for 3.5 miles. The Grove will be on your right.

To reach the trailhead via public transportation from Chicago, take the CTA Blue Line to the Jefferson Park stop, transfer to the Pace Route 270 Milwaukee Avenue bus, and get off at the 1275 N. Milwaukee stop. Walk 0.3 miles north on Milwaukee Avenue to reach the entrance to the Grove.

MACUSHLA BREWING CO.

Sandwiched between a Walgreens drugstore and the longtime Glenview restaurant Hackney's, Macushla is a narrow but charming brewery that was established in 2012 by husband-and-wife team Mike and Megan Welch. Mike, whose grandparents opened Hackney's in 1939, was a homebrewer who dreamed of owning his own brewery, so he left his job as a commodities trader to open Macushla next door to Hackney's. However, just shy of the brewery's one-year anniversary, Mike passed away suddenly, and now Megan runs the brewery, keeping his dream alive. The brewery has a warm community feel and is usually filled with regulars, who in summer months spill outside onto long picnic tables along an alleyway patio. You'll find around a dozen craft beers on the menu, one of which is the Holla-Peno, a clever take on Macushla's LOUminator NEIPA that adds fresh jalapenos. The beer has the citrus flavor and dankness of a great NEIPA, but with a fun, subtle kick of heat that may take a minute to percolate. The refreshing spiciness of the beer pairs nicely with a relaxing walk at the Grove. There's no food on the menu at Macushla, but you can settle down and order in from Hackney's next door or other nearby spots.

LAND MANAGER

Glenview Park District
2400 Chestnut Avenue
Glenview, IL 60026
(847) 724-5670
www.glenviewparkdistrict.org

BREWERY/RESTAURANT

Macushla Brewing Co.
1516 E. Lake Avenue
Glenview, IL 60025
(847) 730-5199
www.macushlabeer.com

Distance from trailhead: 4.6 miles

LAKEWOOD FOREST PRESERVE

EMBRACE THE CALM OF A SECLUDED PATH

NORTHWEST SUBURBS, WAUCONDA, IL

▷··· STARTING POINT	···✗ DESTINATION
EQUESTRIAN TRAIL PARKING LOT	**HERON POND**
🍺 BREWERY	🔳 HIKE TYPE
PHASE THREE BREWING CO.	**EASY**
🐾 DOG FRIENDLY	📅 SEASON
YES	**YEAR-ROUND**
$ FEES	🕐 DURATION
NO	**45 MINUTES**
⛰ MAP REFERENCE	↦ LENGTH
LAKE COUNTY FOREST PRESERVE	**2.2 MILES** (LOOP)
🔍 HIGHLIGHTS	〰 ELEVATION GAIN
SERENE WALKING, HORSES, POND VIEWS	**88 FEET**

**PIXEL DENSITY
HAZY IPA**

 CLOUDY ORANGE

 PINEAPPLE,
SPICES

 ZESTY GRAPEFRUIT

BITTERNESS   SWEETNESS

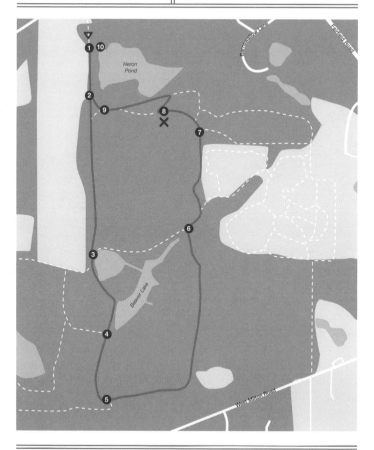

HIKE DESCRIPTION

Find quiet along this secluded equestrian trail, a serene, heavily wooded path where they walk horses, don't they? Then bring on the noise at Phase Three with a bold, hoppy IPA.

Lakewood may be Lake County's largest forest preserve, but from a hiking standpoint, much of it provides only a paved experience, which is better for biking. For this reason, we decided to hike where the horses go.

With more than 2,800 acres of land, Lakewood is a beautiful forest preserve with several fishing ponds. It has a wonderful equestrian trail that offers more peace and solitude than the main trails. This hike takes you deep into gorgeous oak woods, and if you're lucky like we were, you'll spot a horse or two on the trail.

You'll begin the walk just outside the equestrian trail parking lot. This is a separate, secluded lot off Ivanhoe Road. The trailhead, marked with a sign, is easy to find.

You'll begin by going right on a wide, dusty, grassy path, passing Heron Pond on your left. You'll be surrounded by a dense oak forest, however, which makes it hard to see the pond.

The trail is soft under your feet and it's a pleasant walk, a serene stroll with no bikes allowed.

A number of signs will point you along the trail. There are some off-shoot paths that mostly lead to stables. Since it's a horse trail, you'll want to look down from time to time to spot any "road apples" (horse

poop). You might also sight herons, spindly legged sandhill cranes, and chipmunks, and sometimes a stunning horse majestically trotting along.

About midway into the walk, the trail circles away from the pond and brings you deeper into the forest, where blue jays, red-eyed vireos, and cardinals fly about.

Toward the end of the walk, you'll take a hard right down a hill. The path will guide you to a close-up view of Heron Pond, which you couldn't see well before. This offshoot path soon brings you back to the main equestrian path and the parking lot.

TURN-BY-TURN DIRECTIONS

1. Take the wide gravel equestrian trail at the south end of the parking lot.
2. At 0.2 miles, stay straight on the main loop trail.
3. At 0.5 miles, with a small lake on your left, you'll come to two forks. Stay straight at both of them to continue the loop.
4. At 0.7 miles, stay straight at the fork.
5. At 0.9 miles, stay straight at the fork.
6. At 1.5 miles, bear right to stay on the loop.
7. At 1.7 miles, bear left to stay on the loop.
8. At 1.8 miles, bear right for a quick detour to check out Heron Pond. Take a left to walk along the lagoon.
9. At 2.0 miles, bear right to continue on the main loop back toward the trailhead.
10. At 2.2 miles, reach the trailhead.

FIND THE TRAILHEAD

The trailhead is on Ivanhoe Road, just 0.5 miles west of Fairfield Road in Wauconda. To get here from downtown Chicago, take I-90//94 for a little over 8 miles, then keep right at the fork where the highway becomes solely I-94 West. You'll remain on I-94 West for almost 22 miles, then take exit 21 for Half Day Road. Head west on Half Day Road for 7 miles. Turn right on Old McHenry Road and continue for 3 miles. Turn right onto N. Fairfield Rd and continue for 3.3 miles. Take a left onto Ivanhoe Road and continue for 0.5 miles, and you'll see a sign for equestrian parking on your left. Turn down the narrow gravel road, which soon ends at a parking lot and bathroom.

PHASE THREE BREWING CO.

The Phase Three logo, a drawing of what looks like a hummingbird with dotted wings, symbolizes the three phases the owners have gone through with their now lauded brewery. One dotted wing symbolizes phase one—the start of three friends working together, making beer, and designing one-off labels. A second solid-lined wing represents phase two, where the owners took greater steps in learning more about beer, the business and officially starting a brewery beyond homebrews. The colored-in head and tail represent phase three, renting brewery space, owning equipment, and fully operating as a brewery. That third phase puts the brewery in an industrial parking lot in Lake Zurich, Ill. The front room where you order beer is a refined space decorated with the logo and a mural depicting birds. The location also has a back room with a more traditional warehouse feel and pinball machines, TVs, and a lively atmosphere. This is where you can order to-go brews from a large vault of canned beer.

Phase Three is known for its range of booming IPAs, particularly flavorful double dry-hopped IPAs, milkshake IPAs, and ales with bold, spicy flavors. For our hike, the brewery's flagship Hazy IPA, Pixel Density, is a perfect choice. The brewery started with three friends creating beer on the side and has grown into a twelve-tank operation. The owners are currently building a second restaurant and taproom in Elmhurst, Ill.

LAND MANAGER

Lake County Forest Preserves
27277 Forest Park Road
Wauconda, IL 60084
(847) 367-6640
www.lcfpd.org/lakewood

BREWERY/RESTAURANT

Phase Three Brewing Co.
932 Donata Court
Lake Zurich, IL 60047
(630) 393-2337
www.phasethreebrewing.com

Distance from trailhead: 2.7 miles

DEER GROVE FOREST PRESERVE

HIKE ALONG A CREEK AND SEE DEER

NORTHWEST SIDE, PALATINE, IL

▷⋯ STARTING POINT	⋯✘ DESTINATION
DUNDEE ROAD	**STONE BRIDGE**
🍺 BREWERY	🔲 HIKE TYPE
BUFFALO CREEK BREWING	**MODERATE** 🚶
🐾 DOG FRIENDLY	📅 SEASON
YES	**YEAR-ROUND**
$ FEES	🕐 DURATION
NO	**1 HOUR 25 MIN.**
⛰ MAP REFERENCE	↦ LENGTH
FOREST PRESERVES OF COOK COUNTY	**3.5 MILES** (LOOP)
🔍 HIGHLIGHTS	〰 ELEVATION GAIN
DEER SIGHTINGS, HILLY TERRAIN	**102 FEET**

4.5 %
ALCOHOL
CONTENT

BUFFALO GOSE

 CHAMPAGNE YELLOW

 PASSION FRUIT

 TART MELON

BITTERNESS	SWEETNESS

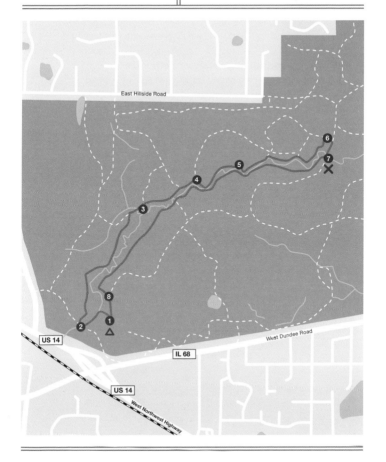

HIKE DESCRIPTION

Observe the deer in Deer Grove, traversing rocky terrain formed by long-ago glaciers. Then kick back at Buffalo Creek Brewing with a tart Buffalo Gose.

At a park called Deer Grove, expectations will be high for seeing, well, deer. This hike delivers. Along the predominantly hilly, heavily forested trek, we saw a handful of deer feeding on grass and quietly moving about the crackling fallen branches. Key to spotting the beautiful creatures is likely choosing to hike the quieter and more rugged Deer Grove West Woodland and Wetland Nature Preserve, one of several sections comprising the nearly 2,000 acres that make up the Deer Grove Forest Preserve.

At the start of our route, a large sign describes the history of Deer Grove and its rolling terrain, which was formed by glaciers during the Ice Age. To the right of the sign is an orange sign for a narrow and inviting path that heads immediately into oak and walnut trees.

You'll pass over uneven, hilly terrain and catch a view of the shallow creek that you'll see repeatedly throughout this hike. Following the narrow dirt path along the creek, you'll soak up the beauty of black and white oak trees. After crossing a bike path, the hike really kicks off.

The wooded trail takes you along a narrow dirt path that rises onto a bluff along the creek but also dips and turns into different tree-lined areas. The path is marked with red and orange paint, which helps you keep an eye out for bumpy tree roots.

Walking along the creek, you may see American toads and brown boreal chorus frogs. It's fun to spot them hiding in the muddy brown stream.

The path rises and falls along the creek. The trees resemble sculptures, and birds such as the white-breasted nut hatch, blue jays, and cardinals wing about.

You'll follow the creek until it hits another bike path at a large stone bridge. This makes for a nice stopping point with a view overlooking the stream. After the bridge you'll head back into the woods for the return trip along the other side of the creek. If you take it quietly, you're likely to see some deer.

TURN-BY-TURN DIRECTIONS

1. At the Deer Grove sign at the north end of the parking lot, take a right and then a quick left onto a small dirt path, marked only by a black wooden post and an orange sign that says "No horseback riding or biking."
2. At 0.2 miles, take a right onto a paved path and then another right to get back onto the small dirt path. You're now on the north side of the creek.
3. At 0.9 miles, just after you cross a small creek, bear slightly right to stay on the path.
4. At 1.1 miles, bear right at the fork to stay along the creek.
5. At 1.5 miles, bear right at the fork to stay along the creek.
6. At 2.0 miles, the small dirt path ends. Take a right onto a wider path and then another right onto a concrete path.
7. At 2.1 miles, cross the creek over the stone bridge and pass a sign saying "Trail open to foot traffic only." Head right onto the small dirt path. You're now on the south side of the creek and will be for the rest of the hike.
8. At 3.5 miles, as the dirt path ends, bear right onto the paved path. The trailhead is just ahead.

FIND THE TRAILHEAD

The trailhead is at the north end of the Deer Grove West parking lot, which is on Dundee Road, just east of Northwest Highway in Palatine and a 40-mile drive from the center of Chicago.

Take Interstate I-90 West for 34 miles to Exit 65 for Roselle Road. Bear right onto Roselle Road and take it for 1.0 miles. Then turn left on Algonquin Road and proceed for 0.9 miles. Bear right on South Ela Road and follow it for 3.3 miles. Turn right onto Dundee Road; the Deer Grove West parking lot is 0.4 miles down Dundee Road on your left.

BUFFALO CREEK BREWING

Buffalo Creek Brewing is a beautiful, Bavarian-style brewery in a stately house on a large plot of land in the quaint, resort-like village of Long Grove. This town of about 8,000 inhabitants is 35 miles from Chicago and has a horse-and-buggy feel, with antique shops and candy stores. The brewery's patio features a military-themed playland for kids, a stage for music, and a rotating food truck. The land backs up to a forest and a trail leads into a small circle of wooded land where guests can walk. The beer lineup is broad and steeped in the classics; we find that the very tart Buffalo Gose, with its strong fruit flavors, fits the easygoing atmosphere of the brewery. Long Grove has a rich German heritage and so does the brewery—developed by owner and brewmaster Mike Marr. The beers are malt-forward, crisp, and classically German.

LAND MANAGER

Forest Preserves of Cook County
536 North Harlem Avenue
River Forest, IL 60305
(800) 870-3666
www.fpdcc.com/downloads/maps/trails/english/FPCC-Deer-Grove-Trail-Map-10-15.pdf

BREWERY/RESTAURANT

Buffalo Creek Brewing.
360 Historical Lane
Long Grove, IL 60047
(847) 821-6140
www.buffalocreekbrewing.com

Distance from trailhead: 6.8 miles

RACEWAY WOODS

BIKING AND WALKING BY AN OLD FOREST RACETRACK

NORTHWEST SUBURBS
CARPENTERSVILLE, IL

▷⋯ STARTING POINT	⋯✗ DESTINATION
WATER TOWER	**THE OLD TRACK**
🍺 BREWERY	HIKE TYPE
SCORCHED EARTH	**MODERATE**
🐾 DOG FRIENDLY	SEASON
YES	**YEAR-ROUND**
$ FEES	⏲ DURATION
NO	**1 HOUR 20 MIN.**
⌂ MAP REFERENCE	↦ LENGTH
KANE COUNTY FOREST PRESERVE	**3.0 MILES** (LOOP)
🔍 HIGHLIGHTS	∿ ELEVATION GAIN
BIKING HILLS, RACETRACK	**259 FEET**

RUGGED COALMINER PORTER

5.9 % ALCOHOL CONTENT

 DEEP BROWN

 COCOA, COFFEE

 ROASTED, NUTTY, COFFEE

BITTERNESS

SWEETNESS

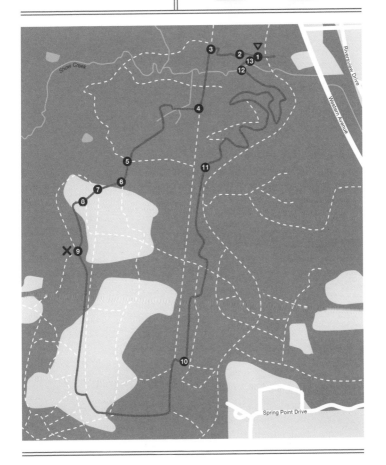

HIKE DESCRIPTION

Take an adventurous walk in a woods with dirt-bike hills and scenic views of a ghostly old racetrack; then make a pit stop and fuel up with a robust porter at Scorched Earth.

More than 120 acres of savanna grass and woodland grounds surround Meadowdale International Raceway, a European-style racecourse that held both sports car and motor races from 1958 until 1969. After the course saw multiple crashes and a fatality, it developed a reputation as a recklessly dangerous track, which likely contributed to its short run.

Now, in its place, is Raceway Woods, complete with steep dirt hills for extreme biking or running and bumpy walking paths that lead deep into the woods. Safe to say, this reimagined use of the grounds comes with some thrill but none of the danger of its previous life.

Start your hike at the Meadowdale Track's original water tower, which sports a vintage gasoline billboard on its large white facade. It's an excellent photo op and stands just at the entrance to the dirt-bike playland.

This open space is filled with hills and dirt paths to race through, but you can walk or run them too. For the hike, steer right and climb a narrow dirt path up a hill and onto a road backed by woods. Head toward the bridge to your left. Once you cross, you'll spy a discreet entrance to the woods. A sign by the start of the woodland path reminds you that you're entering a protected natural area where no bicycling is allowed.

In the woods, you'll hike along an unevenly marked dirt path—often covered by leaves in the fall—but the area is fun and woodsy, and you'll be able to find your own way through it easily.

Once out of the woods, you'll follow a gravel path lined by pine and fir trees, prairie grass, and honeysuckle. There are private residences further down the road, so be neighborly and stay on the path until you come upon the paved circular track of car-racing lore.

Tall grass and weeds fill out the midfield of the track, giving it a rustic, nostalgic beauty. You can walk around the cracked asphalt track, run it, or simply cross it and find your way back onto the rugged biking trails.

Keep an eye (and an ear) out for bikers as you hurry back through the playland of biking trails. It's truly fun to sprint the big dips and ramps to close out your experience.

TURN-BY-TURN DIRECTIONS

1. Follow the path from the trailhead until you reach a fork, then stay straight and follow a small dirt-bike trail.
2. At 0.1 miles, bear right onto another dirt-bike path and follow it up a hill.
3. At 0.2 miles, at the top of the hill, bear left onto a large limestone path and head over a wide footbridge.
4. At 0.4 miles, bear right to leave the wide path and join a small, unmarked hiking trail into the woods and across a small creek.
5. At 0.7 miles, continue on the unmarked trail as it leads up a small hill.
6. At 0.8 miles, once out of the woods, bear right onto a wider gravel path.
7. At 0.9 miles, stay straight at the fork on a slight slope leading into a small evergreen forest.
8. At 1.0 miles, stay straight at the intersection.
9. At 1.3 miles, bear left out of the forest and into a clearing to join the old raceway asphalt track; loop around the track.
10. At 2.0 miles, leave the asphalt track and bear right onto a small dirt-bike path through the woods.
11. At 2.6 miles, stay straight at the fork to remain on the winding dirt-bike path. Follow the zigzags all the way down to the bottom of the hill.
12. At 2.9 miles, head over the bridge and bear right to return to the trailhead.
13. At 3.0 miles, arrive back at the trailhead.

FIND THE TRAILHEAD

Located in Carpentersville, IL, Raceway Woods is roughly an hour's drive from Chicago. Take I-90 West for 39 miles to State Route IL-31 North. You'll take Exit 54B off I-90 West and merge onto IL-31. Drive for 3.5 miles and reach the entrance on your left off IL-31. It is not accessible via public transportation.

SCORCHED EARTH BREWING CO.

There's no better way to refuel after a raceway walk than with a pint of the area's finest motor oil. In fact, Scorched Earth's Rugged Coalminer porter (like many porters and stouts) may pour like motor oil, but it is mild with a nice roasted-coffee flavor. This creamy brew feels like a warm hug, and sipping it at Scorched Earth's woodland brewpub is a real treat. The brewery gets its name from stories about times before Illinois was settled by European colonists, when prairie fires frequently broke out after dry grasslands were struck by lightning or intentionally set ablaze for land development. And just as community and development rose from the ashes, Scorched Earth underwent a similar rebirth. A long-time brewery in the area, it recently went through a change of

ownership and is now under the lead of Greg Doyen. Much of the leg-
acy and feel remains intact, and Scorched Earth is a beautiful, rustic
brewery. Rotating food trucks park near the wide wooden patio that
overlooks a forest, offering a range of food styles. The beer portfolio is
robust, too: a host of ales, IPAs, sours, ciders, Belgian beers, stouts,
porters, and more.

LAND MANAGER

Raceway Woods Forest Preserve
17N702 Western Avenue
Carpentersville, IL 60110
(630) 232-5980
www.kaneforest.com

BREWERY/RESTAURANT

Scorched Earth Brewing Co.
203 Berg Street
Algonquin, IL 60102
(224) 209-8472
www.scorchedearthbrewing.com

Distance from trailhead: 4.1 miles

CRABTREE NATURE CENTER

SOAK UP PRAIRIE, WOODS, AND WETLAND

NORTHWEST SUBURBS, BARRINGTON, IL

▷⋯ STARTING POINT	⋯✕ DESTINATION
VISITOR CENTER	**PHANTOM PRAIRIE TRAIL**
🍺 BREWERY	🏁 HIKE TYPE
WILD ONION BREWERY	**EASY**
🐾 DOG FRIENDLY	📅 SEASON
YES	**YEAR-ROUND**
$ FEES	🕐 DURATION
NO	**1 HOUR 10 MIN.**
⛰ MAP REFERENCE	↦ LENGTH
FOREST PRESERVE OF COOK COUNTY	**3 MILES** (LOOP)
🔍 HIGHLIGHTS	〰 ELEVATION GAIN
WETLAND VIEWS	**91 FEET**

6.5 %
ALCOHOL
CONTENT

PINEAPPLE
MISFIT IPA

 DARK YELLOW,
ORANGE

 PINEAPPLE,
CARAMEL

 CITRUS,
PINEAPPLE

BITTERNESS

SWEETNESS

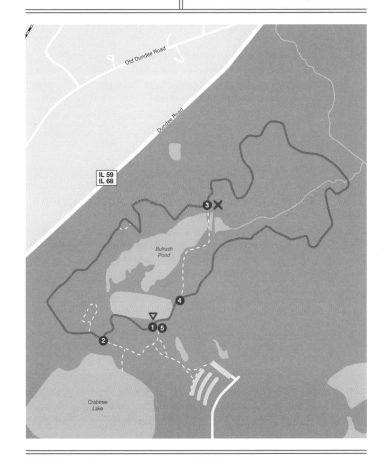

HIKE DESCRIPTION

Woodland, wetland, and prairie come together at the relaxing Crabtree Nature Center. Continue the cozy experience with a refreshing pineapple-flavored beer at Wild Onion's old-style brewhouse.

Crabtree Nature Center is made up of more than a thousand acres of glacial landforms and offers a series of loop trails that connect and highlight the area's varying terrains: a flatland prairie, a robust woodland, and a beautiful wetland where you can spot sandhill cranes.

This is an easy hike and most of the trail is a very wide patch of mowed grassland, much like a concourse for mall walkers.

You'll begin the hike just past the Visitor Center and join a path called Grant's Hollow Trail. The grassy path is surrounded by prairie grass, willows, and cattails and is home to a multitude of different birds. You'll see them flying above the long grass and around Crabtree's many ponds. After a long straight stretch, the path veers left toward three small frog ponds, where toads and bullfrogs play hide-and-seek from hikers.

You'll then take a slightly elevated path into a wooded area and turn right onto the Bur Edge Trail, named for the Bur Oak trees you'll see towering over you. The path features a hideaway activity area with educational exhibits like "guess the age of a tree" and more. You can dip in for a visit or else stay on the path. The Bur Edge Trail then circles through prairie grass and forested areas, where red ferns grow in the fall.

Soon, you'll take a hard left turn off the path and join the Phantom Prairie Trail, which ascends to a quintessential Midwestern prairie. You'll loop around the grassland on this trail until you find yourself back on the Bur Edge Trail, which you'll follow back to the Visitor Center. At the end of the trail, you'll see a paved path that takes you behind the Visitor Center and toward large cages where a great horned owl, a red-tailed hawk, and other impressive birds are on display.

TURN-BY-TURN DIRECTIONS

1. Just past the Visitor Center, bear left onto the Grant's Hollow Trail.
2. At 0.2 miles, bear right onto the Bur Edge Trail (there is a nature play area just up ahead on the right if you are hiking with children).
3. At 1.3 miles, bear left onto the Phantom Prairie Trail.
4. At 2.8 miles, continue straight at the fork to rejoin the Bur Edge Trail.
5. At 3.0 miles, return to the Visitor Center.

FIND THE TRAILHEAD

The Crabtree Nature Center is just over 36 miles from downtown Chicago at 3 Stover Road, Barrington, IL. From the city, get on highway I-90 West and follow it for nearly 32 miles to Exit 62/Barrington Road. Take the exit and then turn right and continue for 3.0 miles to Palatine Road, where you'll turn left. Drive for another mile and then turn right onto Stover Road to enter the preserve. Stay left and wind your way toward the parking lots near a long paved path that leads to the Visitor Center.

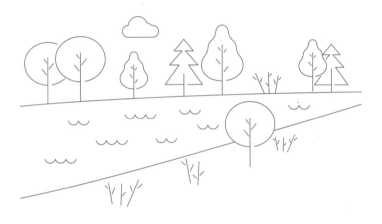

WILD ONION BREWERY

When it began operations in 1996, Wild Onion was one of the first craft breweries in the Chicagoland area. It now distributes to five states in the Midwest. The owners, the Kainz family, operate a 50-barrel brewhouse with nearly 7,500 square feet of warehouse space, and a beautiful banquet center for weddings and events. Based in Lake Barrington, the brewery has strong ties to Chicago proper. The story of the family-owned venture goes back to when the owner's father ran Kainz Dairy in Chicago's Lincoln Park neighborhood in the 1900s and repurposed part of the dairy processing facility in order to brew beer during prohibition. Coincidentally, Wild Onion began its brewing using dairy tanks. Its name is a reference to the region's prolifically growing wild onions. The local Potawatomi tribe even had a word to describe the smell of the wild onions that grow near the wetlands off Lake Michigan: che-cau-gua.

Wild Onion's flagship Misfit IPA was one of the early craft beers to make waves in Chicago and beyond, and the brewery now produces flavored variations. We like the popular Pineapple Misfit, which offers the perfect refreshment after a warm summer walk through Crabtree. Wild Onion is a beautiful brewery, housed in a large brick building that feels like a mid-19th century beer hall. It's also a great restaurant. The extensive menu features soups, salads, wraps, tacos, Bavarian pretzels, and a lot more. It's definitely a great place to refuel after a hike.

LAND MANAGER

Forest Preserves of Cook County
536 North Harlem Avenue
River Forest, IL 60305
(800) 870-3666
www.fpdcc.com/downloads/maps/nature-centers/english/FPCC-Crabtree-Nature-Center-Map-4-17.pdf

BREWERY/RESTAURANT

Wild Onion Brewery & Banquets
22221 North Pepper Road
Lake Barrington, IL 60010
(847) 381-7308
www.onionbrewery.com

Distance from trailhead: 8.3 miles

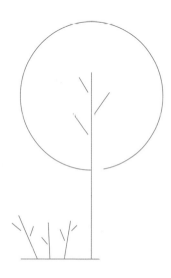

BLACKWELL FOREST PRESERVE

FEEL THE BURN AFTER THIS TRIPLE CLIMB

WEST SUBURBS
WARRENVILLE, IL

▷⋯ STARTING POINT	⋯✕ DESTINATION
BOAT LAUNCH PARKING LOT	**MOUNT HOY TUBING HILL**
🍺 BREWERY	🗺 HIKE TYPE
TWO BROTHERS ARTISAN BREWING	**MODERATE** 🚶
🐾 DOG FRIENDLY	📅 SEASON
YES	**YEAR-ROUND**
💲 FEES	🕐 DURATION
NO	**45 MINUTES**
🗺 MAP REFERENCE	↦ LENGTH
FOREST PRESERVE DISTRICT OF DUPAGE COUNTY	**1.2 MILES** (LOOP)
🔎 HIGHLIGHTS	〰 ELEVATION GAIN
SCALING THE HILL, VIEW ABOVE THE TREES	**274 FEET**

4.5 %
ALCOHOL CONTENT

ASTRO FIZZ SOUR

FLAT,
DARK YELLOW

MANGO,
PINEAPPLE

TROPICAL FRUIT PUNCH

BITTERNESS

SWEETNESS

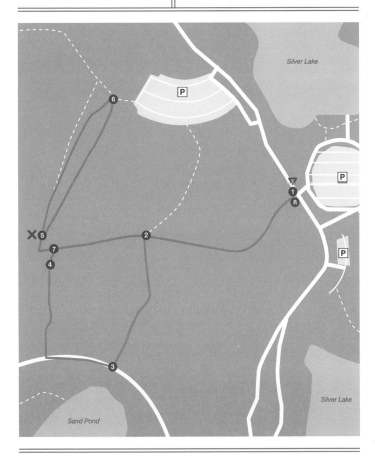

HIKE DESCRIPTION

Enjoy three ways to walk up to a scenic overlook surrounded by beautiful prairie grass and prairie rosen weeds; then give your thighs a rest at Two Brothers with an Astro Fizz fruit punch sour.

There are several ways to enjoy the Blackwell Preserve: on a walk around McKee Marsh, where the skeleton of a woolly mammoth was found in 1977; on paddle boats touring Silver Lake, once a quarry; and on the climb up Mount Hoy.

We'll hike up Mount Hoy, a 150-foot-high hill that makes for thrilling sledding during the snowy winter months. It's also a go-to exercise hill for the community and a beautiful place for birding and walks through prairie grass. There are three paths up the hill; we've crafted a way to access all of them to get a full experience and a workout.

You'll start at the trailhead just across the road from the Boat Launch Parking Lot. This is the lot for Silver Lake, where you'll want to park and maybe rent a paddle boat, canoe, or kayak after the hike for a peaceful lake experience. As you begin the hike, you'll stroll along a gravel path

with the hill ahead of you. About three-fourths of the way up, you'll take a dirt trail that cuts through lush prairie grass, white sweet clover, and prairie rosen weed grass as it heads back down the hill.

The trail emerges onto a road, at the side of which you'll walk along a gravel-and-grass path for 100 feet or so. Then you'll take a dirt trail heading back up. This very steep, narrow trail up the side of the hill is a tough climb, and proper footwear is a must. For extra burn, run it!

At the top, a path swings you back to the main gravel path and onto the summit of Mount Hoy, a circular grass dome. Circle the dome and take in the views of oak and hickory treetops in the distance, Silver Lake, and an archery range; then find your way to the entrance of the Mount Hoy tubing run. This is a very wide grass path that sweeps straight down the hill. We ran it, wind in our faces, pine trees on our right. Just as you catch your breath, you'll duck right and find yet another path up the hill. You'll walk along this path, spotting goldfinches and humming-birds, back up to the top. Then take the main white gravel path all the way down and back out to the lot—and get in that paddle ride.

TURN-BY-TURN DIRECTIONS

1. Take the white gravel path just across the main road from the boat launch sign.

2. At 0.2 miles, halfway up the hill, bear left at the fork on a dirt trail and head downhill.

3. At 0.3 miles, bear left at the main road; then bear right to head up a steep dirt path.

4. At 0.6 miles, bear right at the top of the hill; then take an immediate left onto the white gravel path and head toward the lookout point. Walk the circle path at the top of the hill for the views.

5. At the lookout point at 0.7 miles, take the wide grassy Snow Hill path down the hill.

6. At 0.9 miles, at the bottom of the hill, take the skinnier grassy path next to the wide path back up the hill.

7. At 1.2 miles, at the top of the hill, bear left; then take another left and follow the white gravel path back down the hill.

8. At 1.5 miles, reach the bottom of the gravel path and return to the parking lot.

FIND THE TRAILHEAD

The drive out to Warrenville, Ill., is 32 miles. From downtown Chicago, take I-290 West for 13.6 miles and keep left at a fork to join I-88 West. Continue for a little over 15 miles and take Exit 125 for Winfield Road. Veer right on Winfield Road and then, after 2.0 miles, turn right onto Main Drive. Stay straight on Main Drive (don't bear left onto Slim Beach Road), and the Boat Launch parking lot will shortly be on your right. Main Drive goes uphill and the lot appears just beyond the top of the hill. The trailhead is across the road from the Boat Launch sign at the north end of the parking lot, near the boat rentals.

TWO BROTHERS ARTISAN BREWING

Owned by brothers Jim and Jason Ebel, this brewery started operations in 1996 and became an early leader in the craft beer scene in Illinois. The brewery made its name early with German Hefeweizens, country ales, and sours. It remains a 100%-family-owned brewery and has expanded to include a second location in Aurora, Ill., that hosts an annual music festival. Both locations feature a wide-ranging menu of sandwiches, burgers, chicken wings, and pizza. Two Brothers also roasts its own coffee beans, which get distributed to retailers around the state.

Two Brothers distributes throughout several states in the Midwest. The Ebel brothers have grown their family business into a brewery operation with a 40,000-square-foot facility, a 50-barrel system, and 3,000 barrels of fermentation space. After hiking Mount Hoy, you deserve a

fruit-forward sour ale from this top-tier Illinois brewer—and the Astro Fizz fruit punch sour delivers enough kick and tartness to liven your senses. The adorable, cartoonish, Jetsons-like beer can will take you to the stars. The Mount Hoy hike only takes you up a hill, but it's a refreshing experience either way.

LAND MANAGER

Illinois Department of Natural Resources
3S580 Naperville Road
Wheaton, IL 60189
(630) 933-7200
www.dupageforest.org/hubfs/DuPage2022/Maps/Blackwell-Trail-Map.pdf

BREWERY/RESTAURANT

Two Brothers Tap House
30W315 Calumet Avenue
Warrenville, IL 60555
(630) 393-2337
www.twobrothersbrewing.com

Distance from trailhead: 2.7 miles

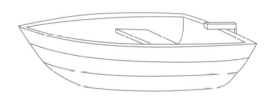

CHICAGO PORTAGE NATIONAL HISTORIC SITE

HIKE THROUGH CHICAGO'S ORIGIN STORY

WEST SUBURBS, LYONS, IL

▷⋯ STARTING POINT	⋯✕ DESTINATION
GRASS PATH TO THE RIGHT OF SHELTER	**OPEN WATER MARSH**
🍺 BREWERY	🔲 HIKE TYPE
BUCKLEDOWN BREWING	**EASY** 🚶
🐾 DOG FRIENDLY	📅 SEASON
YES	**YEAR-ROUND**
$ FEES	🕐 DURATION
NO	**30 MINUTES**
⛰ MAP REFERENCE	⊢ LENGTH
FOREST PRESERVES OF COOK COUNTY	**1.2 MILES** (LOLLIPOP LOOP)
🔍 HIGHLIGHTS	〰 ELEVATION GAIN
MARSH, CHICAGO HISTORY	**5 FEET**

4.5 %
ALCOHOL
CONTENT

CACTUS PANTS
MEXICAN LAGER

CLASSIC GOLD

WHEAT

CITRUS, CORNDS

BITTERNESS

SWEETNESS

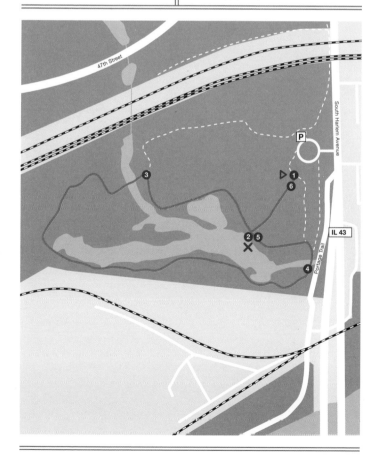

HIKE DESCRIPTION

Visit the birthplace of Chicago on this pleasant walk that takes you to the site of a historical river crossing; then settle in at BuckleDown Brewing for a crisp lager.

It is often said that Chicago wouldn't be Chicago if it wasn't for the Chicago Portage, which links the Great Lakes and the Mississippi River and is the channel Native Americans and explorers used to cross into what became the city of Chicago in the late 1600s. By the 1850s, new waterways, such as the I&M Canal, had been created and the portage became a critical junction for bringing goods and materials into a growing Chicago.

Today, the portage is around 50 acres of beautiful marshland and floodplain forest. And while this isn't a long hike, it provides a unique insight into the origins of modern Chicago. The site earned National Park recognition in 1952 and is part of a 16-mile-long paved trail system called the Salt Creek Trail.

You'll begin in an area just off the parking lot, where signage provides an in-depth history of the portage. There is also a large steel statue commemorating the explorers Father Marquette and Louis Joliet as the first Europeans to cross the portage alongside members of the Kaskaskia American Indian tribe in 1673.

From the exhibit shelter, you'll spot a 10-foot-wide grassy path dotted with stone steps. Follow the path for a short distance until you come upon a sitting area overlooking the marsh, where you'll be treated to a very pretty view of the water and the surrounding duckweed, the world's smallest flowering plant. From the sitting area, turn right onto a

gravel path, which you'll follow around the water's edge. This peaceful narrow path has lovely oak tree coverage, so take your time as you stroll around the pond.

You'll stay the course until you come upon the first of two bridges. This stone and metal bridge offers a pretty overlook of the marsh that was once a swamp and deposits you on another gravel path through the woods. This section of the walk leads through a lovely forest, where you can spot robins and indigo bunting birds.

As the path bends around the water, it narrows and begins to dip and turn. You'll follow this around to the other side of the water. There's plenty of wildlife in the area, so keep your eyes peeled! (We saw a baby deer with her mother grazing in the grass off the edge of the water.)

The path eventually turns away from the water's edge and leads over a sturdy metal bridge, giving you a second overlook of the mossy waters. On the other side, you'll stay left to loop back toward the sitting area and take the wide grass path back to the education area for some final reading.

TURN-BY-TURN DIRECTIONS

1. From the picnic area shelter, take the wide grass path that heads southwest from the parking lot.
2. At 0.1 miles, come to the main gravel loop trail and bear right. (Before you do, walk down to the water's edge for a beautiful view of the marsh.)
3. At 0.3 miles, bear left to head over a bridge and stay on the main loop path.
4. At 1.0 miles, cross the bridge and bear left.
5. At 1.1 miles, you have completed the loop. Bear right to return to the grass path.
6. At 1.2 miles, return to the trailhead to complete the hike.

FIND THE TRAILHEAD

From downtown Chicago, follow I-55 South for 10 miles, then take Exit 283 for IL-43/Harlem Avenue and bear right onto Harlem Avenue. Continue for 0.3 miles and the well-marked entrance will be on your left. Located off Harlem Avenue, south of 47th Street in Lyons, IL, the national site is very easy to spot from the road and instantly welcomes you into a half-moon parking lot facing the sculpture. The trail begins on a grassy path that departs from the covered picnic area just west of the parking lot.

BUCKLEDOWN BREWING

Tucked off a busy street that leads to an industrial part of town, Buckle-Down Brewing is a small taproom built by the owner himself that opened in 2012. Ike and Michelle Orcutt opened the brewery, driven by Ike's passion for homebrewing. Ike learned about larger-scale production under the tutelage of Pete Crowley of Haymarket Brewery and then made his dreams a reality by founding BuckleDown. The brewpub has 15 beers on tap and favors classic styles, such as clean IPAs, pale ales, pilsners, and porters. Our beer of choice is the Cactus Pants Mexican Lager, a remarkably crisp and crushable beer that goes well with a lime wedge and makes for a refreshing finish to the Chicago Portage National Historic Site stroll. BuckleDown uses quirky décor and branding on their cans and merchandise. The beer Clencher is supported by a stick-drawn monster-like creature on cans and very cool sweatshirts. Then, an old-school belt and suspenders cartoon drawing is featured on a can and on BuckleDown trucks in town. Live music, trivia nights, and food trucks bring locals to the taproom, so you'll find no shortage of atmosphere here.

LAND MANAGER

Forest Preserves of Cook County
536 N Harlem Avenue
River Forest, IL 60305
(800) 870-3666
www.fpdcc.com/downloads/maps/trails/english/FPCC-Salt-Creek-Trail-Map-9-16.pdf

BREWERY/RESTAURANT

BuckleDown Brewing
8700 47th Street
Lyons, IL 60534
(708) 777-1842
www.buckledownbrewing.com

Distance from trailhead: 2.1 miles

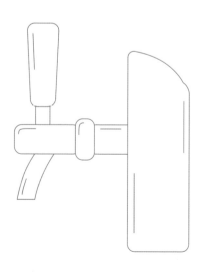

NAPERVILLE RIVERWALK

A LIVELY WALK ALONG THE DUPAGE RIVER

WEST SUBURBS, NAPERVILLE, IL

▷··· STARTING POINT	···✕ DESTINATION
TRAILHEAD NEAR GRAND PAVILION	EASTERN TRAILHEAD
🍺 BREWERY	🔲 HIKE TYPE
SOLEMN OATH BREWERY	EASY 🚶
🐾 DOG FRIENDLY	📅 SEASON
YES	YEAR-ROUND
$ FEES	⏲ DURATION
NO	1 HOUR 30 MIN.
🗺 MAP REFERENCE	↦ LENGTH
SHORTLY AFTER TRAILHEAD ON THE PATH	3.2 MILES (ROUND-TRIP)
🔍 HIGHLIGHTS	〰 ELEVATION GAIN
COVERED BRIDGES, SCULPTURES, MILLENNIUM CARILLON	4 FEET

SNAGGLETOOTH
BANDANA IPA

6.5 %
ALCOHOL
CONTENT

 CLOUDY YELLOW ORANGE

 PINE,
MANGO

DANK,
BITTER PINE

BITTERNESS

SWEETNESS

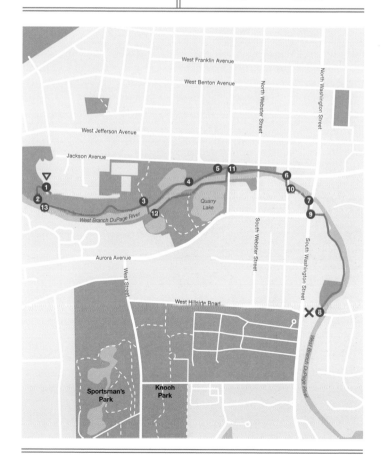

HIKE DESCRIPTION

Take in the sights along the Naperville Riverwalk (and climb the stairs if you dare). Grab a seat inside one of Solemn Oath Brewery's slick A-frame shelters and sip on one of the best IPAs around.

Roughly a two-mile walk along the DuPage River, the Naperville Riverwalk is the pride and joy of the suburb, the third-largest city in Illinois. with nearly 150,000 residents. The riverwalk crosses through the town's liveliest district, home to restaurants, museums, a large community swimming pool, and several memorials and picnic spots. All of this activity makes the riverwalk a fun place to people-watch, but the hike also offers quiet places along the river with cute covered bridges and groves of oak trees.

The hike along the riverwalk takes you up along the river and back, but you'll cross the river a few times to see the sights. You'll start on the far west end of the walk and head east, beginning just beyond a large picnic area called the Grand Pavilion. You'll head off from near where the parking lot ends, where two stone fences and a cobblestone walkway provide convenient access to the woodland trail.

Soon after you head off under the trees, you'll see the large DuPage River to your right; the park and immediate riverside attractions will be on your left. For example, as you walk along, you'll see a large artificial beach and community pool called Centennial Beach.

Shortly after taking in the beach views, you'll come to your first covered bridge. These beautiful wooden structures make a great place for a photo. As you continue along the path, you'll see a massive steel sculpture comprised of several bending, red metal swooshes, which is

called "Landforms" and was crafted by Jack Arnold. The sculpture was gifted to the City and placed along the riverwalk in 1984, three years after it opened. Past the sculpture, you'll come to Eagle Street, which brings you into the hustle and bustle of downtown Naperville.

On the other side of the busy restaurant scene, the hike quiets down again, regaining its beautiful tree-lined views of the river. You'll continue along until you reach the end at the intersection of Hillside Road and Washington Street. Simply turn around here and head back the way you came. You'll cross to the other side of the river at Eagle Street, so you can get an up-close view of the Millennium Carillon in Moser Tower, a nearly 160-foot-tall bell tower that you can see for most of the walk. The tower has 253 steps and 72 bells. We recommend buying a ticket to walk to the top, as this will add to your hike and give you elevated views of the beautiful city and riverwalk. The tower looks like an ornate stone rocket ship, and is just one gem of many to explore along this trail.

TURN-BY-TURN DIRECTIONS

1. Begin the walk on a cobblestone pathway that leads between two stone pillars and fences and into the woods. Take your first left to head toward the river.
2. At 0.1 miles, bear left at the Riverwalk sign to reach the waterside path.
3. At 0.4 miles, bear right at the fork near Centennial Beach. Then take an immediate left to stay along the river (don't cross the wooden bridge here; you'll cross it on the way back).
4. At 0.6 miles, stop for a photo op at the covered bridge (but don't cross here).
5. At 0.7 miles, check out the "Landforms" sculpture by Jack Arnold; then cross Eagle Street to continue the Riverwalk.
6. At 1.0 miles, bear right on Main Street to cross the bridge; then bear left to follow the Riverwalk path.
7. At 1.1 miles, bear right onto South Washington Street and then take a left on Aurora Avenue to continue on the south side of the river path.
8. At 1.6 miles, reach the southern trailhead of the Riverwalk. Turn around and head back the way you came.
9. At 1.9 miles, head back on South Washington Street to cross the river; then continue walking along the river.
10. At 2.1 miles, bear right onto South Main Street and then take a left to continue the Riverwalk on the north side of the river.
11. At 2.7 miles, as a slight detour from the original path, bear left onto South Eagle Street to cross the bridge and then turn right to head west on the Riverwalk. You're now back on the south side of the river.
12. At 2.8 miles, check out the Millennium Carillon in Moser Tower. Then turn right to cross over the wooden bridge. After crossing the bridge, turn left.
13. At 3.2 miles, at the Riverwalk sign, bear right at the fork and then take another right to return to the trailhead.

FIND THE TRAILHEAD

To get to the Naperville Riverwalk from downtown Chicago, take I-290 West for just under 14 miles before merging onto I-88 West. Continue for 13 miles and then take Exit 127 for Naperville Road. Keep left at the fork here and stay straight for about half a mile before turning right onto Diehl Road. After 1.0 miles, turn left onto North Washington Street and stay on it for 2.0 miles. Then, turn right onto Spring Avenue and continue for 0.3 miles before turning left onto Eagle Street. From Eagle Street, turn right onto Jackson Avenue and continue for several blocks until you reach the entrance for the Centennial Beach parking lot. Enter the beach parking lot from Jackson Street, a residential road in Naperville. Stay straight on the entry road until you reach Sindt Memorial Court. Take a right and continue until the road's end. Park for free at the far western point of the lot near the trailhead. The hike begins on a cobblestone path that leads between two stone pillars and fences at the western edge of the parking lot near the Grand Pavilion, at 912 Honorary Sindt Memorial Court in Naperville.

SOLEMN OATH BREWING

Snaggletooth Bandana is right up there with the best of the IPAs Chicago has to offer, and the Naperville taproom tops the list of unique brewery experiences. Taken together, the beer and the brewery make for a great end-of-hike treat (especially if you climbed the bell tower stairs). After your efforts, you've certainly earned a taste of some of Solemn Oath's noteworthy IPAs.

The taproom's interior has a standard warehouse feel, with tables surrounded by working tanks. The brewery's patio, however, is anything but ordinary: It is set up like a campground with fireplaces, fake pine trees, rows of chopped wood, and artsy A-frame structures. The patio is called the Solemn Oath Beer Camp and Garden and begs to be visited in the colder months (though it's pretty great in summer, too). The brewery has grown and now also boasts a Chicago location. While its menu is pretty IPA-heavy, it also includes some seasonal lagers.

LAND MANAGER

TED Business Group
400 South Eagle Street
Naperville, IL 60540
(630) 420-4108
www.naperville.il.us/globalassets/media/brochures
/riverwalk-brochure.pdf

BREWERY/RESTAURANT

Solemn Oath Brewing.
1661 Quincy Avenue, Suite 179
Naperville, IL 60540
(630) 995-3062
www.solemnoathbrewery.com

Distance from trailhead: 2.5 miles

WATERFALL GLEN

A TEN-MILE HIKE AND WATERFALL DIP

SOUTHWEST SUBURBS.
DARIEN, IL

▷⋯ STARTING POINT	⋯✗ DESTINATION
MAIN ENTRANCE TRAILHEAD	**ROCKY GLEN WATERFALL**
🍺 BREWERY	🗺 HIKE TYPE
BLACK HORIZON BREWING CO.	**DIFFICULT**
🐾 DOG FRIENDLY	📅 SEASON
YES	**YEAR-ROUND**
$ FEES	🕐 DURATION
NO	**4 HOURS 15 MIN.**
⛰ MAP REFERENCE	↦ LENGTH
AT THE TRAILHEAD	**10.1 MILES** (LOOP)
🔍 HIGHLIGHTS	〰 ELEVATION GAIN
WATERFALL, SAWMILL CREEK BLUFF	**404 FEET**

KEY LIME
FISTFIGHT IPA

 BURNT ORANGE

 GRAHAM CRACKER,
VANILLA

 KEY LIME,
VVANILLA

BITTERNESS   SWEETNESS

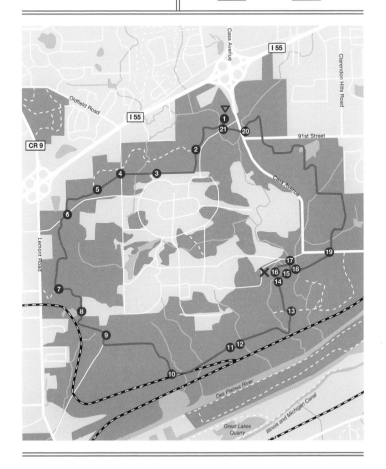

HIKE DESCRIPTION

Take a long walk through marshland and mature forest and cap it off with a waterfall view and a dip in a rocky stream. Get your just desserts with a key lime–flavored beer at Black Horizon Brewing.

The modest waterfall and rocky stream below it may be the main attraction of Waterfall Glen, an area that locals flock to and treat like a swimming pool, but the park is not named after this aquatic feature. In fact, it's named after Bud "Seymour" Waterfall, an early board president of the forest preserve district.

Regardless, the 2,500-acre preserve is easily one of the most impressive in Illinois, and its soft limestone gravel path and varying oak, hickory, and shagbark forest views make for a worthy 10-mile trek (you can run or bike it, too).

The hike begins on an easy-to-follow limestone gravel path. However, not long into the hike, you'll spot a wide, all-grass path on your left cutting right through the deciduous forest. You'll take this, the Tear-Thumb Trail, which runs along a tall barbed-wire fence protecting the Argonne National Laboratory—a high-level physics and computer science research lab run by the Department of Energy and originally part of the Manhattan Project. (You may get some "Stranger Things" vibes walking through a stunning forest past a top-secret government facility.)

Leaving the Tear-Thumb Trail, you'll take a left out of tall grass and back onto the limestone path. You'll pass beautiful cattails and marshland and soon find yourself under a canopy of massive oaks. This mature forest has a grander feel than many other forest-preserve walks.

About a third of the way into the walk, the tree coverage thins, and you'll experience a long sunny walk along Kettle Woods, an area formed by glaciers 10,000 years ago. You'll pass a section of land mowed for flying model aircraft and then the Musk Turtle Marsh overlook, from which you can see turtles, egrets, and 6-foot-tall reeds of canary grass.

At about the halfway point, you'll walk alongside train tracks and spot a stone wall dating back to 1921. This was part of a nursery that belonged to Chicago's Lincoln Park Commission and once supplied shrubs, willows, and elms to the Chicago lakefront.

You'll also see the Sawmill Creek Bluff, home to a sawmill and quarry in the 1800s, and get a nice view of the creek below funneling toward the waterfall. While there are some dirt paths that cut down to the stream to reach the waterfall, we'll stay on the limestone path and reach the falls on the Rocky Glen Trail.

At the bottom of the artificial waterfall, it's fun to kick off your shoes and walk through the refreshing water. Many people wear swimsuits and wade directly into the waterfall. You may see crawfish and jumping water bugs. Be careful, as it's a rocky stream and you can hurt your feet.

Leaving the waterfall, you'll get back on the limestone path, which connects back to the main path. Around nine miles in, you'll come upon another gorgeous pond with marsh wrens sounding their click-clack birdcall.

This walk is long but rich in beautiful sights: hickory trees, oaks, goldenrod, wild bergamot flowers, wiry spikerush weeds, and oat grass. Overall, it's an amazing journey through an old forest with nearly 350 species of plant life—and the waterfall dip is fun, too!

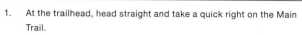

TURN-BY-TURN DIRECTIONS

1. At the trailhead, head straight and take a quick right on the Main Trail.
2. At 0.5 miles, bear left onto a grassy path called the Tear-Thumb Trail.
3. At 1.1 miles, keep straight to stay on the Tear-Thumb Trail.
4. At 1.4 miles, keep straight.
5. At 1.7 miles, head straight to rejoin the Main Trail.
6. At 2.1 miles, take a right and then a quick left to stay on the Main Trail.
7. At 3.0 miles, bear left at the fork.
8. At 3.5 miles, reach the marsh lookout point.
9. At 3.8 miles, bear right, pass an information board, and continue on the trail.
10. At 4.6 miles, bear left at the signage to stay on the Main Trail.
11. At 5.3 miles, reach the site of the former Lincoln Park Nursery.
12. At 5.4 miles, take a left and then a quick right.
13. At 6.2 miles, bear left at the sign to stay on the Main Trail.
14. At 6.6 miles, bear right at the Sawmill Creek overlook.
15. At 6.7 miles, turn left onto the Rocky Glen Trail for a quick detour to see the Rocky Glen Waterfall. Then take another quick left at the trail marker.
16. At 7.0 miles, reach the Rocky Glen Waterfall; then head back the same way you came.
17. At 7.2 miles, bear right on the Rocky Glen Trail.
18. At 7.3 miles, bear left to rejoin the Main Trail. (Just ahead in the parking lot, you can refill your water bottle at the pumping station.)
19. At 7.7 miles, cross Bluff Road to stay on the Main Trail.
20. At 10.1 miles, cross Cass Avenue to stay on the trail through some woods; then cross North Gate Road.
21. At 10.4 miles, bear right to return to the trailhead.

FIND THE TRAILHEAD

The Waterfall Glen main entrance parking is on the north side of North-gate Road, a quarter-mile west of Cass Avenue. This is important to note, as there are three parking lots for the park and some aim to get hikers closer to the waterfall. The main entrance lot leads to the long 10-mile hike.

From downtown Chicago, head to I-290 West toward the west suburbs and take it for 0.4 miles before staying right and joining I-90 East/I-94 East. Proceed for 1.5 miles and then exit onto I-55 South toward St. Louis, also known as the Stevenson Expressway. After 20 miles, take Exit 273A for South Cass Avenue. After roughly a mile, you'll see signs for Waterfall Glen and Argonne National Laboratory; hang a quick right onto South Frontage Road and go up a small hill and into a parking lot. Drive toward the bathrooms; the main trailhead is right at the edge of the lot.

BLACK HORIZON BREWING CO.

After a strenuous hike in the sun, a refreshing beer is on the agenda, and Black Horizon delivers with its fruit-forward Fist Fight series of flavored IPAs with a hefty beer base. Key Lime Fist Fight, a hazy IPA with pureed key lime and vanilla brewed in, packs a tart, delicious flavor. The brewery also makes a peach-flavored Fist Fight. Both beers use the staple Fist Fight IPA as its foundation and then add in some exciting flavors. The brewery also has a cherry cheesecake–inspired beer, a blood-orange sour, and rye-based lagers. These are big bold beers for a small microbrewery with a dozen rotating beers on tap and a small selection of canned beers to go.

Three friends operate the brewery (Charles St. Clair, Kevin Baldus, and Alex Stankus) in an industrial park, where they brew and can on-site. The taproom is fun with a neon-lit bar, foosball, and arcade games. It's decorated with wild skull-based art in line with some of the can designs. Also notable: The brewery is one of only four Black-owned breweries in Chicago.

LAND MANAGER

Forest Preserve District of DuPage County
3S580 Naperville Road
Wheaton, IL 60189
(630) 933-7200
www.dupageforest.org/hubfs/DuPage2022/Maps/Waterfall-Glen-Trail-Map.pdf

BREWERY/RESTAURANT

Black Horizon Brewing Co..
7560 South Quincy Street
Willowbrook, IL 60527
(630) 413-4964
www.blackhorizonbrewing.com

Distance from trailhead: 3.3 miles

LITTLE RED SCHOOLHOUSE
NATURE CENTER

NATURE CLASS IS IN SESSION

SOUTHWEST SUBURBS, WILLOW SPRINGS, IL

▷··· STARTING POINT	···✗ DESTINATION
OUT FRONT OF THE VISITOR CENTER	**SITE OF THE ORIGINAL SCHOOLHOUSE**
🍺 BREWERY	🎲 HIKE TYPE
POLLYANNA BREWING	**EASY**
🐾 DOG FRIENDLY	📅 SEASON
NO	**YEAR-ROUND**
$ FEES	🕐 DURATION
NO	**1 HOUR**
⛰ MAP REFERENCE	↦ LENGTH
NEAR VISITOR CENTER	**2.7 MILES** (THREE LOOPS)
🔍 HIGHLIGHTS	〰 ELEVATION GAIN
WILDLIFE SIGHTINGS, SITE OF 1886 SCHOOLHOUSE	**158 FEET**

6.8%
ALCOHOL
CONTENT

ELEANOR PORTER

  BLACK

  SMOKY

  CARAMEL,
COFFEE

BITTERNESS

SWEETNESS

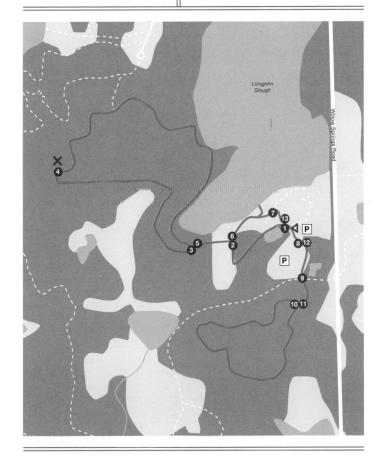

HIKE DESCRIPTION

Head back to school on a stroll through gorgeous woods steeped in educational history. Then, enjoy a recess at Pollyanna Brewing, where you can sample a tasty porter fittingly named after Eleanor Porter, author of the 1913 children's novel *Pollyanna*.

The Little Red Schoolhouse Nature Center has a lively energy and is sure to give you that warm, first-day-of-school buzz. In fact, there is so much going on here that, when you step out of your car, you may not know where to go first. You can follow the crowds flowing into the multi-level, interactive Visitor Center, stroll around it to visit the resident barred owl or red-tailed hawk, head straight for the historic schoolhouse from which the nature center gets its name, or explore the Accessible Garden, a 6,000-square-foot expanse of landscaped greenery and bright flowers built for people of all physical abilities to enjoy. The garden features interpretive signage and an ADA-compliant concrete walkway that is about half a mile long.

The nature center has a rich history. The original schoolhouse was built in 1886, far back in the woods, and provided traditional schooling to generations of children. It was moved off-site in 1932, and then rebuilt at its current site behind the Visitor Center in 1952, when it opened as a nature school for kids and adults.

Historical significance aside, it's a beautiful place to spend an afternoon. For this hike, you'll explore all three loop trails—the Farm Pond Trail, the Black Oak Trail, and the White Oak Trail.

You'll begin in front of the Visitor Center, just to the left of an oversized wooden chair that makes for a perfect photo op. Take the unmarked path to begin the Farm Pond Trail, which you'll follow past the center's apiary. Here you'll encounter the trail's first educational signage, which tells you everything you need to know about the Center's bees.

From there, you'll join the Black Oak Trail and wrap around Longjohn Slough Lake, where you're likely to see turkey vultures flying overhead and great white egrets resting in the shallow water.

At almost one mile in, deep into the beautiful woods, you'll come to the original site of the Little Red Schoolhouse (where it sat from 1886 to 1938). You'll then loop back to the lake to complete the Black Oak Trail and pick up the Farm Pond Trail where you left off.

At nearly two miles in, you'll walk past the center and take a crosswalk through the parking lot to begin the third and final loop—the White Oak Trail. This is the center's least traveled and quietest trail. Once past a marsh with yet another educational sign about the local fauna, you'll meet the larger Palos Trail System—a nearly 6-mile unpaved hiking and bike trail that takes you through neighboring forest preserves.

For this hike, you'll stay straight on the White Oak Trail, which takes you on a serene stroll through a gorgeous oak forest, where you may hear the song of a Scarlet Tanager (in the family of the cardinal—the Illinois state bird). You'll loop back around to find yourself back in the parking lot you set off from, where this educational chapter will come to a close.

TURN-BY-TURN DIRECTIONS

1. Begin the hike at the unmarked trail entrance in front of the Visitor Center, just to the left of the giant wooden chair.
2. At 0.2 miles, bear left to begin the Black Oak Trail.
3. At 0.3 miles, bear right to begin the loop.
4. At 0.9 miles, stop at the original site of the schoolhouse.
5. At 1.4 miles, bear right.
6. At 1.5 miles, bear left to join the unmarked Farm Pond Trail and shortly afterward turn onto the gravel path on your left to reach a lookout point over the lake. When you're done, return back to the main path.
7. At 1.6 miles, return to the Visitor Center and bear right. Head past the large wooden chair where your hike began and continue straight to cross a crosswalk through the parking lot.
8. At 1.7 miles, at the sign for the White Oak Trail, take the gravel path and stay right to begin the trail.
9. At 1.8 miles, the trail intersects with the Palos Trail System Trail; stay straight at the fork to continue on the White Oak Trail.
10. At 1.9 miles, bear right to begin the loop.
11. At 2.4 miles, reach the end of the loop. Bear right to continue, then head straight at the next fork.
12. At 2.6 miles, continue straight at the crosswalk through the parking lot.
13. At 2.7 miles, return to the giant chair in front of the visitor center to complete the hike.

FIND THE TRAILHEAD

To get to the nature center, located at 9800 Willow Springs Road, Willow Springs, IL, from downtown Chicago, take I-55 South for about 15 miles and then take Exit 279A for US-45 South/South La Grange Road. Head south for about 3 miles, then bear right onto West 95th Street and continue for just over a mile. Bear left onto Lavin Road/Willow Springs Road and continue for 0.6 miles; the nature center will be on your right. The hike begins on the Farm Pond Trail, which starts in front of the Visitor Center, just to the left of the giant wooden chair. Note that the trail is unmarked.

POLLYANNA BREWING AND DISTILLING

While Pollyanna now operates four suburban brewpubs and a distilling business, the company began with its brewing facility in Lemont, IL in 2014. The elegant establishment overlooks the historic I&M Canal and sits among lively businesses and restaurants in this quaint suburb that feels more like a small town. Feel free to order food from the nearby restaurants and bring it into the brewery, where we recommend the year-round Eleanor Porter, a rich brown beer. It's the perfect pairing for a schoolhouse hike, and the German hops and caramel notes are nice,

too. Pollyanna also carries a range of lagers, experimental wheat beers, a series of hefty barrel-aged beers, IPAs, pale ales, and even a malt liquor. Including seasonal brews, its portfolio boasts more than 30 beers. The company's distilling operation is located at its St. Charles, IL, location, and produces rum, vodka, gin, wormwood-infused liquor, bourbon, aquavit, and more.

LAND MANAGER

Forest Preserves of Cook County
536 North Harlem Avenue
River Forest, IL 60305
(800) 870-3666
www.fpdcc.com/downloads/maps/nature-centers/english
/FPCC-Little-Red-Schoolhouse-Nature-Center-Map-4-17.pdf

BREWERY/RESTAURANT

Pollyanna Brewing and Distilling
431 Talcott Avenue
Lemont, IL 60439
(630) 914-5834
www.pollyannabrewing.com

Distance from trailhead: 8.4 miles

LAKE RENWICK HERON ROOKERY

THIS HIKE IS FOR THE BIRDS

SOUTHWEST SUBURBS,
PLAINFIELD, IL

▷··· STARTING POINT	···✕ DESTINATION
VISITOR CENTER	**ROOKERY GAZEBO**
🍺 BREWERY	🁫 HIKE TYPE
WERK FORCE BREWING CO.	**EASY** 🚶
🐾 DOG FRIENDLY	📅 SEASON
YES	**AUGUST 16TH–FEBRUARY 28TH**
$ FEES	🕐 DURATION
NO	**1 HOUR 20 MIN.**
🗺 MAP REFERENCE	⊢ LENGTH
AT THE TRAILHEAD	**3.0 MILES** (TWO LOOPS)
🔍 HIGHLIGHTS	〜 ELEVATION GAIN
ROOKERY VIEWS, LAKE BUDDE VIEW	**0 FEET**

5.0 %
ALCOHOL
CONTENT

WERKTOBERFEST
MARZEN LAGER

RICH COPPER

BREADY CARAMEL

BISCUITS,
MALT

BITTERNESS   SWEETNESS

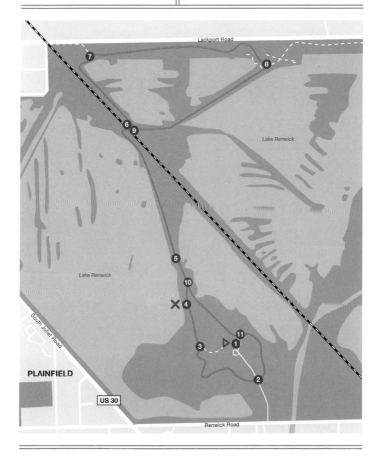

HIKE DESCRIPTION

Enjoy a quiet hike around the Lake Renwick Rookery; then toast the islands at island-themed Werk Force Brewing with a Werktoberfest.

The hallmark of the Lake Renwick Preserve is an artificially constructed rookery spread across a series of small islands in the middle of Lake Renwick. A path takes you to an overlook where a high-powered viewing lens helps you get a closer look at nesting birds. The rookery is a multi-level wooden structure that has been described as an apartment complex for nesting birds. There are three floors or levels in the rookery. Double-breasted cormorants and blue herons nest on the top floor. Egrets tend to nest on the second level, and the bottom floor is the favored residence of castle egrets and black-crowned night herons. Bald eagles, pelicans, and more than 200 other species of birds have been recorded at the migratory station. The trail leading to this bird haven, as well as the trails around it, offer a wonderfully unique outdoor experience.

On this hike, you'll walk two loop tails—the unpaved Heron Rookery Trail and the paved Lake Renwick Bikeway—that are connected by a long straightaway.

You'll begin the hike just behind the small one-room visitor center. There's a large map at the trailhead, which two paths depart from. You'll take the path on the right (the Heron Rookery Trail) and join a limestone walkway that guides you through poplars and cottonwoods. The trail circles back behind the parking lot, so wave hello to your car and then cross the entrance road and veer onto a more densely forested path. Here, elm trees grow amid a rare kind of horsetail grass that looks like tall, green bamboo.

You'll stay on this path and turn left toward a straightaway limestone path, where a gazebo becomes visible up ahead. This straightaway is framed on either side by tall hazel and elm trees. Despite the lush plant life lining the path, you can sneak views of Lake Renwick on your left and Darter Pond on your right. You'll also spot birds flying overhead toward the rookery.

Once at the gazebo, you'll see the rookery far out in the water—bring binoculars or try one of the free viewing lenses. It may take some patience to find the birds, but once you do, you'll be treated to the sight of egrets, heron, and cormorants. The gazebo also includes some educational information about the birds and rookery.

When you've had your fill of bird watching, you'll exit the gazebo on the far side to rejoin the straightaway path. As you continue, you'll come across several trails leading down to the water for more views of the rookery, and they're worth exploring.

The straightaway path turns onto a larger bike path loop (called the Lake Renwick Bikeway) for the next portion of the hike. This bike path is year-round, but the rookery access path is only open from mid-August through February to protect the nesting habitat of the birds.

Soon, on the paved portion of the hike (there's a cut-grass path on the edges of the bike path to enable you to stay safely out of the way of cyclists), you'll see views of another water system, Budde Lake, with its swans and turtles. The bike-path portion leads through trees to a quaint fishing pier and then continues around the path back to the limestone Heron Rookery Trail. Here, you'll regain the straightaway and then veer left to head back to the trailhead. The hike flies, and you'll spend much of it looking up and watching the splendid birds circle, dive, and soar overhead.

TURN-BY-TURN DIRECTIONS

1. At the trailhead sign, bear right onto the Heron Rookery Trail.
2. At 0.2 miles, stay straight at the fork.
3. At 0.5 miles, bear left at the fork.
4. At 0.7 miles, stop at the gazebo to view the rookery habitat. Continue straight, then bear left and head north on the straightaway.
5. At 0.8 miles, bear left onto a small gravel path to head to the lake for a great view of the rookery.
6. At 1.2 miles, after you emerge from under the railroad tracks, bear left to begin the Lake Renwick Bikeway loop.
7. At 1.4 miles, bear right at the fork to continue the loop.
8. At 1.9 miles, stop at the Budde Lake overlook, then take a quick right to continue the loop.
9. At 2.4 miles, you've completed the Lake Renwick Bikeway loop. Stay straight to get back on the Heron Rookery limestone path.
10. At 2.8 miles, stay straight at the fork.
11. At 3.0 miles, return to the trailhead.

FIND THE TRAILHEAD

From downtown Chicago, take I-90/94 and head east for a mile before merging onto I-55 South to Joliet. Drive on I-55 South for nearly 37 miles. You'll then take Exit 257 to US-30 West, also known as Joliet Road, and continue for about three-fourths of a mile before turning right onto McClennan Avenue. This is a small street that takes you through a residential area before running into Renwick Road. You'll see the entrance to the preserve directly across the street. Take a quick right and then an immediate left to enter the preserve and drive a short distance right into the only parking lot around. You'll see the trailhead map just beyond a short, squat visitor center.

WERK FORCE BREWING CO.

Located roughly two miles from the Lake Renwick Heron Rookery, Werk Force Brewing, with its tropical, tiki-lounge vibes and classic industrial taproom, has a lively brewery atmosphere. The brewery has 15 beers on tap, plus two guest ciders and a collaboration beer. There are slushies that fit the brewpub's Hawaiian theme, and a dedicated section for its lager pours. One of these is the smooth and sweet Werktoberfest, a malty marzen in the Octoberfest style. The beer is one of the brewery's flagship brews and is generally available during the rookery season. In addition to the lagers, you'll find some pale ales and a coffee stout. The beers are the work of brewmasters Brandon Wright, Jake LaDuke, and Jake Scheufler. Food is provided by an on-site kitchen operated by Happy Belly, which serves Hawaiian cheese bread and flatbreads, among other Hawaiian dishes. There's a range of sweet desserts and flavored sodas, too. A large outdoor patio adds nicely to the open taproom layout, which features repurposed barrels as tables.

LAND MANAGER

Forest Preserve District of Will County
17540 West Laraway Road
Joliet, IL 60433
(815) 727-8700
www.reconnectwithnature.org/preserves-trails/visitor-centers/
lake-renwick-heron-rookery-visitor-center/

BREWERY/RESTAURANT

Werk Force Brewing Co.
14903 South Center Street
Plainfield, IL 60544
(815) 531-5457
www.werkforcebrewing.com

Distance from trailhead: 2.0 miles

ORLAND GRASSLAND

STROLL THROUGH A RESTORED ILLINOIS PRAIRIE

SOUTH SUBURBS, ORLAND PARK, IL

▷⋯ STARTING POINT	⋯✕ DESTINATION
167 STREET ENTRANCE AND PARKING LOT	**TAN PRIMITIVE TRAIL**
⬚ BREWERY	⬚ HIKE TYPE
SOUNDGROWLER BREWING	**EASY**
🐾 DOG FRIENDLY	📅 SEASON
YES	**YEAR-ROUND**
$ FEES	🕐 DURATION
NO	**1 HOUR 30 MIN.**
⚠ MAP REFERENCE	⊢ LENGTH
FOREST PRESERVES OF COOK COUNTY	**4.0 MILES** (LOOP)
🔍 HIGHLIGHTS	〰 ELEVATION GAIN
BIRDWATCHING, WILDFLOWERS	**192 FEET**

BIKE SHORTS GRAPEFRUIT RADLER

3.5 % ALCOHOL CONTENT

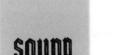

 LIGHT CHAMPAGNE

 CITRUS, TROPICAL

 STRONG GRAPEFRUIT

BITTERNESS   **SWEETNESS**

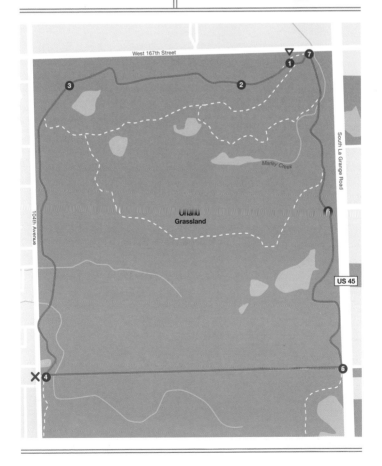

HIKE DESCRIPTION

Stroll a grassy trail and bike path through a beautifully restored open prairie. Following your stint on the bike path, order a Bike Shorts at Soundgrowler.

Walking through the center of the 960-acre prairie of Orland Grassland feels a bit like going back in time to when there were only native plants and animals on the Illinois prairies—and this is no accident. The original prairie was drained and turned into farmland in the early 1900s, but thanks to the efforts of the US Army Corps of Engineers Chicago District, the Forest Preserve of Cook County, and local volunteers, the grassland has been restored and the prairie is as it once was, complete with ancient plant species.

The entire grassland is surrounded by a 5-mile paved bike trail, and there are a few unpaved trails that take you across the prairie itself. For this hike, you'll combine two trails—the outer Red Paved Loop, which loops around past wetlands and through oak savanna forests, and the Tan Primitive limestone path, which cuts straight through the middle of the open prairie.

From the parking lot, you'll take an unmarked grass path that will lead you directly onto the Red Paved Loop bike trail. As you hike west, you'll hear resident birds, such as eastern meadowlarks and common yellowthroats. The grassland is a must-visit for bird lovers—more than 190 species of birds have been sighted here.

As you loop around the northwest corner of the park, you'll enter a beautiful wooded area, one of just a few in the grassland. Head south, and after roughly two miles on the bike path, you'll bear left onto a grassy gravel walking path at a sign that says, "Ecological Management Site." This is what the website map calls the "Tan Primitive Trail," and it cuts straight through the center of the grassland, from west to east.

As you head away from the sounds of nearby traffic and cyclists' chatter, you'll find yourself in a truly remote and isolated field. Towering sunflowers and colorful wildflowers fill the rolling landscape, and it's a stunning miles' walk through the prairie.

When the path ends, you'll rejoin the paved trail and pass through a second woodland area and along a large wetland pond with egrets soaring overhead. The path will then loop you through the prairie and back to the parking lot.

TURN-BY-TURN DIRECTIONS

1. Take the unmarked grassy path at the northwest corner of the parking lot; then take a quick left onto the Red Paved Loop and head west.

2. At 0.1 miles, stop at a sign on the left-hand side of the trail to read about the history of the prairie and check out a sculpture. Return to the trail and continue west.

3. At 0.8 miles, come to the northwest corner of the loop and an entrance from the road. Continue straight on the main loop.

4. At 1.8 miles, bear left onto a grassy gravel path at a sign that says Ecological Management Site. Begin the Tan Primitive Trail that takes you through the prairie.

5. At 2.8 miles, as the grassy gravel path ends, bear left to rejoin the Red Paved Trail.

6. At 3.4 miles, keep straight at the fork.

7. At 4.0 miles, bear left to return to the parking lot.

FIND THE TRAILHEAD

From downtown Chicago, take 55 South for about 15 miles, then take Exit 279A for US-45 S/South La Grange Road and continue on US-45 S/South La Grange Road for about 13 miles. Bear right onto 167th Street, and you'll soon see the entrance for Orland Grassland on your left. The trail begins on an unmarked grassy path in the northwest corner of the parking lot at the 167th Street entrance, which is at the corner of 167th Street and South La Grange Road in Tinley Park, IL.

SOUNDGROWLER BREWING

After you've had your fill of peace and quiet on the Illinois prairie, head into the thundering guitar music of Soundgrowler Brewing, a heavy metal–inspired brewery with delicious Mexican street food and a housemade michelada. Painted skulls and spooky decor fill the spacious taproom, which also has a nice outdoor patio despite being located in an industrial park. Two Mexican lagers are the menu highlights: The flagship Tortilla Hands is mixed with Jarritos grapefruit soda to create a super-refreshing radler variation called Bike Shorts. The concoction is a fantastic summer drink. The brewery also makes seltzers, so there are more refreshing, lighter options at the brewery than you might expect from a metal-themed bar. Maybe metalheads have a soft side, after all. IPAs, pale ales, a doppelbock, and a marzen are also on the taplist, and the brewery has a great community feel with a gorgeous event space connected to the taproom. The location offers truly unique events such as metal yoga, metal Bingo, a broom-making workshop, a sculpting class, Lucha Libre wrestling, and much more.

LAND MANAGER

Forest Preserves of Cook County
General Headquarters
536 North Harlem Avenue
River Forest, IL 60305
(800) 876-3666
www.fpdcc.com/places/locations/orland-grassland

BREWERY/RESTAURANT

Soundgrowler Brewing
8201 183rd Street, Suite P
Tinley Park, IL 60487
(708) 263-0083
www.soundgrowler.com

Distance from trailhead: 2.9 miles

GOODENOW GROVE NATURE PRESERVE

CONNECTING TRAILS THROUGH A CAMPING HUB

SOUTH SUBURBS,
BEECHER, IL

▷··· STARTING POINT	···✕ DESTINATION
OUTSIDE PLUM CREEK NATURE CENTER	**OAK RIDGE TRAIL**
🍺 BREWERY	🔀 HIKE TYPE
EVIL HORSE BREWING CO.	**EASY**
🐾 DOG FRIENDLY	📅 SEASON
NO	**YEAR-ROUND**
$ FEES	🕐 DURATION
NO	**1 HOUR 10 MIN.**
🗺 MAP REFERENCE	↦ LENGTH
FOREST PRESERVE DISTRICT OF WILL COUNTY	**3.2 MILES** (THREE LOOPS)
🔍 HIGHLIGHTS	〰 ELEVATION GAIN
BIRD HOUSES, SNAPPER LAKE	**295 FEET**

LUG WRENCH LAGER

CLEAR WHITE STRAW

HERBACEOUS

MALT-FORWARD, RICE

BITTERNESS

SWEETNESS

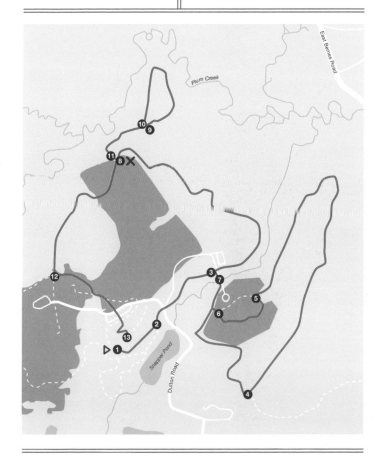

HIKE DESCRIPTION

Be good and visit the campground trails of Goodenow Grove; be evil and indulge in a refreshing lager at Evil Horse Brewing.

Goodenow Grove is widely known to be a great spot for camping, a reputation that dates back to its beginnings as a resident site for Boy Scouts. It's still common to encounter large groups of scouts setting up camp in the area; in fact, you're likely to come across their tents every so often when walking the various offshoot trails of the Plum Creek Greenway Trail in the nature preserve. As this hike combines four of the preserve's trails, you're sure to spot at least a few campsites.

Plum Creek is also the name of the nature center, which is a great place to visit before you start hiking. The highly interactive center features a beehive, a bluebird nest viewing area, a dedicated bird sanctuary and feeding area, and a livestream of the birding area. There are snakeskins and animal skulls on display, an extensive library, and much more.

To begin the hike, look for a limestone path and a trailhead sign for the Plum Creek Greenway Trail, located just a few steps from the nature center. The path leads you behind the center and to the other side of Snapper Pond, which has a circumference of about a mile and is home to many turtles.

You'll soon cross a two-way street and head away from the pond and toward a heavily forested area of oak and hickory trees. It is not uncommon to see rows of tents and grills set up in the open field before the entrance to the woods. After passing through this portion of rich, beautiful tree coverage, you'll come to the first offshoot trail, the High Point Trail. This is a wide grassy path, an equestrian trail that opens up onto expansive prairie grass. The trail soon swaps woodland for two bunny hills that you'll dip down and climb up. Keep an eye out for the birdhouses along the path, welcoming cardinals, blue jays, and more.

High Point Trail is a loop, so follow it all the way to find your way back to the main path, which you'll continue on until you reach another off-shoot trail called the Scout Trail. Here, you'll transition from limestone and grass to a gravel path that loops through beautiful woods and connects you to the Oak Ridge Trail, a short but very woodsy path along a creek. This section gives you the quintessential dirty-trail experience and exposes you to unusual plant life, such as the endangered spotted coral-root orchid and ear-leafed foxglove.

The Scout Trail eventually loops back to the main pathway with its paved finish and into big open fields that are a favorite spot for picnics and gatherings. As you pass through the fields, you'll come in view of the parking lot and the nature center (and a massive hill that's a popular winter sledding spot).

TURN-BY-TURN DIRECTIONS

1. Behind the Plum Creek Nature Center, bear left onto the limestone Plum Creek Greenway Trail.
2. At 0.1 miles, keep straight at the fork.
3. At 0.3 miles, bear right to stay on the limestone path and pass the camping ground.
4. At 0.6 miles, bear left to take the High Point Trail.
5. At 1.4 miles, bear left.
6. At 1.5 miles, bear left and then turn right to get back onto the Plum Creek Greenway.
7. At 1.6 miles, cross the bridge and bear right across the road; head through a parking lot to the Scout Trail trailhead. Head straight on the turf trail.
8. At 2.2 miles, bear right onto the dirt Oak Ridge Trail.
9. At 2.4 miles, stay straight at the fork.
10. At 2.6 miles, complete the loop and bear right to continue on the main trail.
11. At 2.7 miles, bear right to return to the Scout Trail.
12. At 3.0 miles, bear left onto the unmarked Plum Creek Greenway Trail.
13. At 3.2 miles, return to the nature center.

FIND THE TRAILHEAD

To get to the nature preserve by car from Downtown Chicago, take I-90 E/I-94 E for 7.0 miles and stay left to continue on I-94 for 15.0 miles. Take exit 74A-74B for IL-394 S toward Danville and continue on IL-394 S for 14.0 miles. Bear left onto W. Goodenow Road and continue for 1.2 miles, then bear left onto Dutton Road and continue for 0.5 miles. Turn left to enter the nature preserve. Follow signs for the Plum Creek Nature Center. The trail begins on the wide limestone path behind the Plum Creek Nature Center.

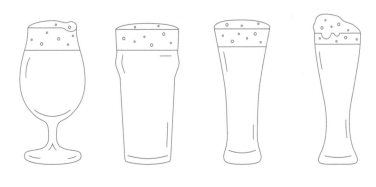

EVIL HORSE BREWING CO.

In 2015, Evil Horse renovated the first floor of a building with deep historical roots in the town of Crete. The two-floor structure was constructed in 1911 as a grain, flour, and feed business. The top floor was used for dances and roller skating. Over the years, the building evolved to house various businesses, from an insurance agency to a barbershop. In the 1940s, a bowling alley took over the top floor. Evil Horse commemorates the building's history by displaying the original bowling alley sign as the centerpiece of its warm and welcoming interior. There's nothing evil about this brewery, but its unbridled passion for beer is certainly on display. The brewery hosts live music and events, has pinball machines and games, and channels the strong community spirit that surrounds it. It serves German-inspired ales and pilsners on the lighter side as well as the extremely crisp and smooth Lug Wrench Lager. The beer uses German and American hops and has a remarkably clear color.

Evil Horse *does* have a dark side though—at least in the way of a series of heavy-hitting beers, including its creamy stout, an Imperial IPA with an ABV in the double digits, a doppelbock with an ABV of 8.5%, and a saison at over 7%. Evil Horse is named for an appaloosa mare owned by the brewmaster that regularly succeeded in bucking off riders. The brewery carries that horse's legend onward. No food is served at the brewery, but the former bowling alley upstairs is now a restaurant that you can order a great pizza from.

LAND MANAGER

Forest Preserve District of Will County
17540 West Laraway Road
Joliet, IL 60433
(815) 727-8700
www.reconnectwithnature.org/preserves-trails/preserves
/goodenow-grove

BREWERY/RESTAURANT

Evil Horse Brewing Co.
1338 Main Street
Crete, IL 60417
(708) 304-2907
www.evilhorsebrewing.com

Distance from trailhead: 6.1 miles

MIDEWIN NATIONAL TALLGRASS PRAIRIE

LEG THE LARGEST OPEN SPACE AROUND

SOUTHWEST SUBURBS, WILMINGTON, IL

▷⋯ STARTING POINT	⋯✕ DESTINATION
PRAIRIE CREEK WOODS TRAILHEAD	**PRAIRIE CREEK BRIDGE**
🍺 BREWERY	🎴 HIKE TYPE
RT 66 OLD SCHOOL BREWING	**EASY** 🚶
🐾 DOG FRIENDLY	📅 SEASON
YES	**YEAR-ROUND**
$ FEES	🕐 DURATION
NO	**1 HOUR**
⛰ MAP REFERENCE	↦ LENGTH
IN THE VISITOR CENTER	**2.5 MILES** (LOOP)
🔎 HIGHLIGHTS	〰 ELEVATION GAIN
VIEWS OF TALLGRASS PRAIRIE, THE OLD TREE	**5 FEET**

5.5% ALCOHOL CONTENT

WILDCAT CREAM ALE

BURNT ORANGE, COPPER

CARAMEL

BUTTER COOKIE, MALT

BITTERNESS   SWEETNESS

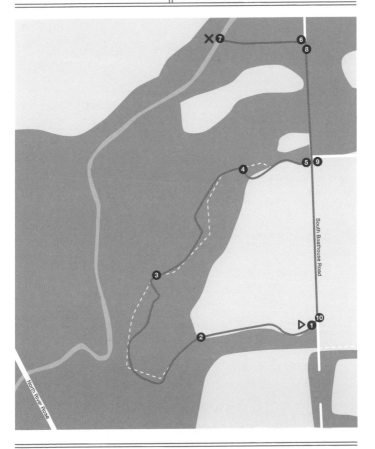

HIKE DESCRIPTION

Walk around the first tallgrass prairie in the country, a former US Army munitions factory turned nature space. Celebrate the Wilmington Wildcats football team with a Wildcat Cream Ale from Rt 66 Old School Brewing.

A clever restoration of more than 20,000 acres of land once occupied by Joliet Arsenal and its munitions factories and ammunitions bunkers, Midewin National Tallgrass Prairie is the first designated tallgrass prairie in the US. It's also the largest open space and island of protected land in the Chicago area. The restoration was no easy feat and required cleaning up years of contaminants left behind by the munitions factories. Today, Midewin boasts 33 miles of trails and includes a special reserve for bison.

On this hike, you'll follow the Prairie Creek Woods Trail loop, which leads through tallgrass that can be over 5 feet high and includes some woodland sections. At the top of the loop, we added in a worthwhile detour to check out the creek the trail was named after (and maybe even stop for a little picnic).

You'll set off from the north end of the River Road Trailhead parking lot and head through a gate on a trail that leads along a wire fence until you reach River Road, where you'll turn right. This takes you to the trailhead of the Prairie Creek Woods Trail. You'll know you're in the right place when you see the beautiful tallgrass. In the fall, the tallgrass is a marvelous gradient of reddish strands that shade into golden yellow and are accented by milkweed plants.

After walking along the grassland for a while, you'll veer into a wooded area known as Prairie Creek Woods. Local legend says it once was a savanna, but that when the land was used as an arsenal, cherry and elm trees grew up, soon to be joined by oak trees and eventually by

non-native osage orange trees and honeysuckle, which invaded the new woodland. There are also more than 35 species of wildflowers in the woods, including Woodland Phlox and Sweet Joe-Pye Weed.

You'll continue hiking through the woods on a dirt-covered path that winds around to an overlook for mossy Buttonbush Pond, which is home to many turtles. Another key stop worth making is to see the oldest tree in the preserve, a large oak that takes four people to wrap arms around.

On this part of the hike, you'll catch glimpses of a hunting stand in the woods, a reminder that hunting is allowed at certain times in Midewin— so it's smart to wear orange if hiking during hunting season.

Back on the gravel path, you'll head north on River Road and then west for a quick detour to check out Prairie Creek, a lovely shaded area that's a perfect spot to rest. Once you've enjoyed some time by the creek, head back to River Road and follow it south through the prairie back to the trailhead.

TURN-BY-TURN DIRECTIONS

1. From the trailhead on River Road, turn left onto the Prairie Creek Woods Trail to begin the hike.
2. At 0.2 miles, stay left to head into the woods.
3. At 0.6 miles, stop at the lookout point for Buttonpush Pond.
4. At 0.9 miles, stop to visit the large oak tree, the oldest tree in the preserve.
5. At 1.0 miles, at River Road, instead of bearing right to complete the loop, you'll bear left to begin the detour up to the creek.
6. At 1.3 miles, bear left at the first fork to head west toward the creek.
7. At 1.5 miles, arrive at the creek and a large wooden bridge. Stop for a rest or picnic by the creek. When you're done, turn around and head back the way you came.
8. At 1.7 miles, bear right at the fork to follow River Road.
9. At 2.0 miles, at the fork, keep straight to stay on River Road.
10. At 2.5 miles, arrive back at the Prairie Creek Woods Trail trailhead to complete the hike.

FIND THE TRAILHEAD

Midewin is a 60-mile drive from downtown Chicago. Take I-55 South for about 55 miles, then take Exit 241 and bear left onto North River Road. Follow this for 1.7 miles and then bear left onto Kankakee River Road (Boathouse Road) and continue for 0.3 miles. The gravel parking lot is on your right, beside a public restroom. Park at the northernmost point of the lot, walk through the gate at the fence and then take the short trail back to River Road. Bear right onto River Road and the trailhead will be on your left.

RT 66 OLD SCHOOL BREWING

Trained in their craft by a brewer friend in Florida, Rt 66 Old School Brewing's beer-passionate owners Steve and Tina Nelson fulfilled a dream by opening a brewery in their hometown of Wilmington, IL. The Nelson's tapped Paul Bidne, an award-winning brewer who cut his teeth homebrewing and at the Flossmoor Station Brewery, to be their master brewer. The brewery has a family-owned vibe and features a game room that will make you feel like you're hanging out in your favorite uncle's basement. The TVs are tuned to sports channels and there are more than a dozen beers on tap, with just about every style covered—from hazy IPAs to saisons, wheat ales, sours, porters, and Berliner Weissbier. The brewery is a fun place to relax after a day spent exploring Midewin's treasured tallgrass. We recommend the deliciously creamy Wildcat Cream Ale. It scores a taste touchdown with its light-bodied, toasty notes—the football reference honors the can, which has a simple photo of two hands hoisting an Illinois High School Association state football championship trophy (the wildcat is the mascot of the local high school team). The can is different from every other crazy cartoon can with a punny name—it's so earnest and heartfelt that you can't help but adore it, much like the brewery itself.

LAND MANAGER

Midewin National Tallgrass Prairie
30239 South State Route East 53
Wilmington, IL 60481
(815) 423-6370
www.fs.usda.gov/Internet/FSE_DOCUMENTS/fseprd551074.pdf

BREWERY/RESTAURANT

Rt 66 Old School Brewing
110 Bridge Street
Wilmington, IL 60481
(815) 476-2220
www.rt66oldschoolbrewing.com

Distance from trailhead: 3.1 miles

DAY TRIPS

SEVEN BRIDGES TRAIL

SCALE BLUFFS AND STROLL BRIDGES IN MKE

SOUTH MILWAUKEE, WIS.

▷··· **STARTING POINT**

SEVEN BRIDGES TRAILHEAD SIGN IN GRANT PARK

···✕ **DESTINATION**

CLIFF OBSERVATORY NO.2

🍺 **BREWERY**

ENLIGHTENED BREWERY CO.

🗺 **HIKE TYPE**

DIFFICULT

🐾 **DOG FRIENDLY**

YES

📅 **SEASON**

YEAR-ROUND

$ **FEES**

NO

🕐 **DURATION**

60 MIN.

⛰ **MAP REFERENCE**

MILWAUKEE COUNTY PARKS

↦ **LENGTH**

2.5 MILES (LOOP)

🔍 **HIGHLIGHTS**

BEACH, BLUFF, RAVINE

〜 **ELEVATION GAIN**

200 FEET

**KETTLE LOGIC
AMBER ALE**

CLEAR COPPER

CARAMEL

MALTY DARK GRAINS

BITTERNESS

SWEETNESS

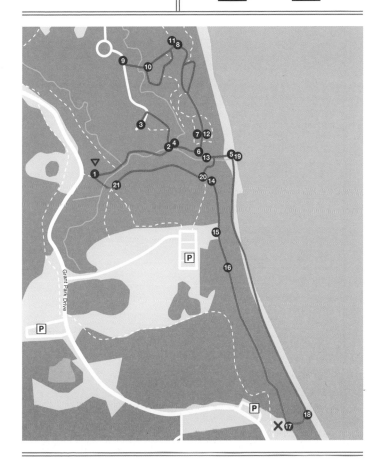

HIKE DESCRIPTION

Choose your own adventure on this Lake Michigan beach-and bluff-hike with a lot of stairs, sand, and bridges. See the light with a grounded amber ale at Enlightened Brewing, a lively brewery in Milwaukee's hippest neighborhood.

For many Chicagoans, the quaint lake towns and campgrounds of Wisconsin offer weekend getaways for a fix of the great outdoors. There are rafting, hunting, and fishing opportunities, as well as antique shops and a Main Street vibe. But Milwaukee (MKE) also works as a fast and fun day-trip destination—offering this under-the-radar, adventurous hike 90 minutes from Chicago.

The hike is the Seven Bridges Trail inside Grant Park, a Milwaukee County Parks destination in the town of South Milwaukee.

The hike is named for the bridges you'll traverse across a ravine, but the big adventure is ascending stairs to various trails along the bluff overlooking Lake Michigan. It's important to note that none of these

trails are marked, and the experience has a choose-your-own-adventure appeal: there are several offshoot trails along the way to dip in and out of. There's no wrong experience traversing the ravine, bluffs, and beach, but we have charted a path that provides a full park experience.

The trail starts near a covered bridge marked by the prophetic words, "Enter this wild wood and view the haunts of nature." There are bathrooms on the other side of the covered bridge, but our hike starts before the bridge at a large trailhead sign providing some history about the Seven Bridges Trail, which was constructed in the 1930s. Instead of heading straight to cross the bridge, take the path just to the left, which begins with stone steps that immediately take you east to some first bridges and through a gorgeous, rocky ravine.

Soon you'll take a quick jaunt up wooden steps to explore Wulff Lodge, the original residence of Frederick Wulff, the former superintendent of Grant Park who lived here in 1917. Next, back down the steps and across bridges, you'll walk to the beach on Lake Michigan. After that, it's up several Lannon-stone stairs to traverse the northern bluff trails overlooking the lake. Along this dirt path among beech, sugar maple, and birch trees there are many offshoot trails, but ultimately you'll want to loop back down into the ravine, where you'll scale more stairs to explore the southern bluff. This long stretch is a remarkable part of the hike, a thin woodsy path right along the edge of the bluff. The lake views are magical, and this part of the walk is very isolated compared to the other section, which is often crowded with beachgoers.

You'll walk this path to Observatory No. 2, an overlook with a rock path down to the beach. The rocks are covered in wire and rubber to provide traction, but the climb down is still difficult. You'll be rewarded, however, when your toes hit sand and you walk back north along the beach. Skip rocks and enjoy the rushing waves until you reach the first beach again. Finally, you'll head back up more stairs and finish strong on forest trails and across the covered bridge. This time you'll see a different sentence inscribed on the bridge: "May the God given peace of this leafy solitude rest upon and abide with thee." Hikers abide.

TURN-BY-TURN DIRECTIONS

1. At the trailhead, instead of crossing the covered bridge, take the path off to the left and head down stone stairs to begin the unmarked hike.
2. At the fork at 0.2 miles, bear sharply left up a winding staircase to check out Wulff Lodge.
3. At 0.3 miles, arrive at the lodge; then head back down the stairs to the trail.
4. At 0.4 miles, back at the bottom of the stairs, head straight over a single bridge to get back on the main trail and head toward the beach.
5. At the fork at 0.5 miles, head straight to check out the beach.
6. After you've left the beach, head back the way you came, but don't cross the bridge. Past the bridge, bear right up stone steps and head up to the north bluffs.
7. At the top of the stairs, you have three options; head straight.
8. At 0.7 miles, bear left, walk down steps, cross the bridge, and head up some more steps.
9. At 0.8 miles, arrive at the picnic grove and children's play area. Then head down the steps, cross the bridge, and head up the steps on the other side.
10. At 0.9 miles, at the top of the steps, bear right for a quick loop.
11. At 1.0 miles, bear right to get back on the path; then take another quick left.
12. At 1.2 miles, back at the three-way fork, head straight down the stone steps.
13. At the bottom of the steps, bear left and then quickly right to head over the big bridge. Take the stone steps up to explore the southern bluffs.
14. At 1.3 miles, bear sharply left at the top of the steps.
15. At 1.4 miles, pass the picnic grove on your right and continue straight.
16. At 1.5 miles, keep left to stay on the narrower path.
17. At 1.7 miles, at an open field with a bench and an overlook (Cliff Observatory 2), bear left to go down a small, steep dirt trail.
18. Bear left and walk along the beach.
19. At 2.2 miles, reach the main beach again, bear left to head over the big bridge and take the stone steps back up.
20. At 2.3 miles, bear right at the top of the steps.
21. At 2.5 miles, bear right over the covered bridge and reach the trailhead.

FIND THE TRAILHEAD

Grant Park is a large park with a golf course and several meeting places. To find the Seven Bridges Trail, park in the lot near S. Lake Drive and Park Avenue. From Chicago, the drive is 84 miles down Interstate 94 West/Milwaukee. Once you enter Wisconsin, look for exit 319, College Avenue, and turn right. You'll drive on the road for a little over two miles and turn right onto S. Lake Drive. Park Avenue is about a third of a mile down; turn left to enter the park and arrive at a line of parking spaces facing the trailhead beside a covered bridge.

ENLIGHTENED BREWING CO.

A striking, sunlit warehouse space in Bay View—arguably Milwaukee's hippest neighborhood—Enlightened Brewing is a joy to visit. The taproom has pinball machines, board games, a Nintendo Wii, and other parlor games to keep you busy for hours. But you'll want to reserve some time to go shopping down the nearby "K Streets" of the neighborhood. Enlightened opened its doors in 2013 and has rotating IPAs, stouts, and cream ales anchoring its list, but one of its flagship beers is a very tasty amber ale. Kettle Logic's earthy flavor is a great follow-up to a hike spanning land and sea; it's very flavorful and creamy with a malty finish. There's no food at the brewery, but plenty of great places to order in from or visit nearby as you explore Bay View and enjoy this fun day trip to MKE.

LAND MANAGER

Grant Park
100 E. Hawthorne Avenue
South Milwaukee, WI 53172
(414) 762-1550
https://county.milwaukee.gov/files/county/parks-department/
Park-Maps/7bridgesmap.pdf

BREWERY/RESTAURANT

Enlightened Brewing Co.
2020 South Allis Street
Milwaukee, WI 53207
(414) 239-8950
www.enlightenedbeer.com

Distance from trailhead: 7.2 miles

STARVED ROCK STATE PARK

VIEW STUNNING CANYONS IN A NATIONAL LANDMARK

UTICA, IL

▷⋯ STARTING POINT	⋯✗ DESTINATION
BEHIND VISITOR CENTER	**HENNEPIN CANYON OVERLOOK**
🍺 BREWERY	🏔 HIKE TYPE
OBSCURITY BREWING AT LODI TAP HOUSE	**DIFFICULT**
🐾 DOG FRIENDLY	📅 SEASON
YES	YEAR-ROUND
$ FEES	🕐 DURATION
NO	**4 HOURS 15 MIN.**
⌂ MAP REFERENCE	↦ LENGTH
POSTED AT TRAILHEAD	**10.8 MILES** (ROUND-TRIP)
👁 HIGHLIGHTS	〰 ELEVATION GAIN
CANYON WALKS, BLUFF VIEWS	**1,336 FEET**

GRAPE POP CULTURED GOLDEN ALE

 4.0 % ALCOHOL CONTENT

 DARK PURPLE

 GRAPE CANDY, FRUITY

 GRAPE SODA POP

BITTERNESS

SWEETNESS

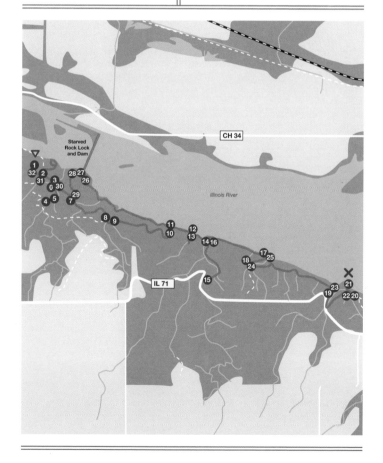

HIKE DESCRIPTION

Canyon views, multiple waterfalls, and the tragic history of rival Native American tribes unfold in this hike. Posthike, enjoy a beer that tastes like grape soda from Obscurity Brewing.

Starved Rock is a crown jewel of hiking in Illinois, a destination park with campsites, lodges, and log cabins, highly regarded dining, and event spaces. It's a major attraction and can draw massive crowds, so be aware. On the hiking side, it delivers 13 miles of trails and 18 canyons. That's 18 stunning formations thanks to glaciers and streams that eroded sandstone into miles of sculptured rock. On this trek, you'll walk nearly 11 miles and see the highest profile canyons.

In 1966, Starved Rock was designated a National Historic Landmark. It earned its name from a battle among rival Native American tribes. The legend goes that in 1760, members of the Illinois tribe hid on the tall rock over the Illinois River from the Ottawa tribe, who were seeking vengeance over the death of their leader, Chief Pontiac. Trapped on the rock, the Illinois died of starvation.

At the start of the hike, stop at the Visitor Center and get a free paper map. Out the back doors of the Center, you'll see a wide path and a trailhead sign for an array of canyons. You'll start by following the sign to French Canyon. It's best to do this hike early to avoid large crowds. The goal is less than a mile from the trailhead, so many hikers make quick in-and-out visits, hoping to see the majestic, 45-foot-tall waterfall. If it hasn't rained recently, however, the fall is often no more than a trickle.

The way to French Canyon leads along a pretty, forested trail that takes you to a set of stone steps and a tight squeeze between large rock formations. The view then opens up to a huge canyon. Then, it's onward to Wildcat Canyon, home to a 90-foot waterfall, on a beautiful hike along the Bluff Trail through white pines and cedars. The Bluff Trail brings you high above the canyon and there are tragic accidents here every year, so take care to maintain a respectful distance from the edge.

The crowds tend to fade and the hike becomes more peaceful once you've passed Wildcat Canyon. You'll head along a mountainous path and then along the River Trail toward the circular-walled Tonty Canyon. You'll be walking right next to the Illinois River (a major waterway, 270 miles long). We saw snakes and cranes on the River Trail, and it can be buggy under the trees.

You'll approach LaSalle Canyon and its rushing waterfall on a narrow, twisting trail beside sandstone walls. After looping up to this canyon, you'll get back on the River Trail, from which you'll take a huge staircase back to the Bluff Trail and the solitude of Hennepin Canyon. This is a somewhat difficult climb through tangled roots, but is relatively unpopulated.

You'll run into crowds again at the Lover's Leap overlook. This site commemorates a legend among the rival tribes according to which a couple forbidden to be together, Romeo and Juliet–style, chose to leap to their deaths from the rocky cliffside of the Illinois River. From here, Starved Rock itself is visible just up the river. You'll continue walking toward it, stopping off to see another great view at Eagle Cliff. From there, it's down wooden steps and up a long, steep path to Starved Rock.

TURN-BY-TURN DIRECTIONS

1. Begin the hike at the trailhead sign on a path behind the Visitor Center.
2. At 0.1 miles, stay straight at the fork and follow signs for French Canyon.
3. At 0.3 miles, continue straight to French Canyon.
4. At 0.5 miles, stop and explore French Canyon.
5. At 0.6 miles, stay straight.
6. At 0.8 miles, bear right.
7. At 1.0 miles, bear right toward Pontiac and Wildcat Canyons.
8. At 1.3 miles, arrive at Wildcat Canyon. Bear left at the boardwalk for a quick photo at the lookout point and then continue along the trail. Take a quick left at the sign for Sandstone Point.

9. At 1.5 miles, bear right to stay on the Bluff Trail towards Sandstone Point and LaSalle Canyon.
10. At 2.4 miles, reach Lone Tree Canyon and take the stairs down to join the River Trail.
11. At 2.5 miles, at the bottom of the stairs, bear right.
12. At 2.7 miles, bear right to hop off the River Trail for a detour into Tonty Canyon; then go back the way you came.
13. At 2.9 miles, bear right to get back on the River Trail.
14. At 3.0 miles, bear right to head toward LaSalle Canyon.
15. At 3.7 miles, reach the waterfall at LaSalle Canyon. Then head back toward the River Trail.
16. At 4.4 miles, bear right to continue on the River Trail.
17. At 4.9 miles, the River Trail ends. Bear right to join the Bluff Trail and walk up the stairs toward Hennepin Canyon.
18. At 5.2 miles, stay straight to remain on the Bluff Trail.
19. At 5.9 miles, curve to the right to stay on the Bluff Trail toward Hennepin Canyon. There are no rails here, so beware of the steep drop-off.
20. At 6.2 miles, bear left onto a small hiking trail.
21. At 6.4 miles, reach the Hennepin Canyon overlook. Then head back to the Bluff Trail.
22. At 6.6 miles, bear right to continue on the Bluff Trail.
23. At 6.9 miles, curve to the left to stay on Bluff Trail.
24. At 7.5 miles, stay straight to continue on the Bluff Trail.
25. At 7.8 miles, bear left at the bottom of the stairs on the River Trail, which you'll follow for the remainder of the hike.
26. At 9.4 miles, bear right to head up the stairs. At the top of the stairs, bear right to head to the Eagle Cliff overlook.
27. At 9.6 miles, arrive at the Eagle Cliff overlook. Then head back— but don't go down the stairs—to continue on the River Trail toward Lover's Leap.
28. At 9.8 miles, reach Lover's Leap. Continue on the River Trail.
29. At 10.0 miles, bear right toward the Visitor Center.
30. At 10.2 miles, continue straight.
31. At 10.4 miles, bear right and head up more stairs to see Starved Rock; then head back the way you came.
32. At 10.8 miles, at the bottom of the stairs, bear right to return to the trailhead.

FIND THE TRAILHEAD

The trailhead is behind the Starved Rock State Park Visitor Center, which is at 2678 E. 873 Road in Oglesby (please note that this is different from the Starved Rock Lodge). To get there from downtown Chicago, take I-90 E/I-94 E to I-55 S/Stevenson Expressway and continue on I-55 S for 42 miles. Take Exit 250B to merge onto I-80 W toward Iowa and continue for 45 miles. Take Exit 81 for IL-178 toward Utica/La Salle; bear left onto IL-178 and continue for 3.4 miles. Once you pass downtown Utica, bear left at the sign for Starved Rock State Park and continue for 0.8 miles; then turn left into the Visitor Center parking lot.

OBSCURITY BREWING AND LODI TAP HOUSE

A short distance from Starved Rock is a beer-loving bar and grill called Lodi Tap House and, across the street, a seasonal sister brewery called Obscurity Brewing—both owned by Illinois Crafted Hospitality Group. Both places are great to visit after a long hike. Lodi Tap House is a burger joint that also serves up wings, wraps, and giant pretzels, but has made its name serving cutting-edge local beers, including beers from Obscurity. The bar also works with breweries around the state to create its highly touted Beer Advent Calendar (24 different Illinois craft beers for the 24 days leading up to Christmas).

Across the street, Obscurity Brewing features a dedicated beer garden, a stage for live music, and a handful of taps. It's only open during the warm months, but Lodi can supply the goods for the rest of the year. The perfect beer after a hike to Starved Rock is the refreshing Grape Pop Cultured Beer. This golden ale is far from golden: it's a deep, dark purple that tastes remarkably close to grape-flavored soda. Obscurity also makes orange and strawberry versions. The brewery has traditional pale ales, a pilsner, red ale, hefeweizen and more, but also two fantastic braggot IPAs made with buckwheat honey.

LAND MANAGER

Illinois Department of Natural Resources
One Natural Resources Way
Springfield, IL 62702
(217) 782-6302
www.starvedrocklodge.com/wp-content/uploads/2019/10/Starved-Rock-Trail-Map.pdf

BREWERY/RESTAURANT

Obscurity Brewing Bier Garten on the I&M Canal
101 Mill Street
North Utica, IL 61373
(815) 667-4324
www.illinoiscrafted.com

Distance from trailhead: 4.5 miles

MATTHIESSEN STATE PARK

TUNNEL THROUGH CAVES IN A DAMP CANYON

OGLESBY, IL

▷⋯ STARTING POINT	⋯✗ DESTINATION
RIVER AREA PARKING LOT	**CASCADE FALLS**
🍺 BREWERY	HIKE TYPE
TANGLED ROOTS BREWING CO.	**MODERATE**
🐾 DOG FRIENDLY	SEASON
YES	**YEAR-ROUND**
$ FEES	⏲ DURATION
NO	**2 HOURS 30 MIN.**
⛰ MAP REFERENCE	↦ LENGTH
ILLINOIS DEPT. OF NATURAL RESOURCES	**6 MILES** (ROUND-TRIP)
🔍 HIGHLIGHTS	〰 ELEVATION GAIN
GIANT'S BATHTUB, DEVIL'S PAINT BOX	**1729 FEET**

DEVIL'S PAINT BOX IPA

GOLDEN AMBER

ORANGES

EARTHY, PINE

BITTERNESS | SWEETNESS

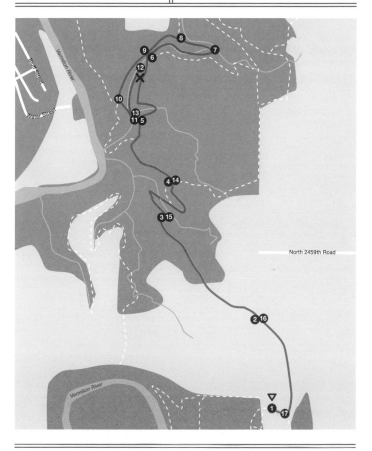

HIKE DESCRIPTION

 Visit the waterfalls and cool and airy caves of the Illinois state park that is home to the Devil's Paint Box, a muddy pit the color of the devil at the base of a canyon. Then cheer your overlord with a Devil's Paint Box IPA from nearby Tangled Roots Brewing Co.

Matthiessen State Park is a fun-filled neighbor of the magnificent Starved Rock State Park and resort. Both feature glacier-formed canyons, waterfalls, and stunning trails, but Matthiessen delivers on a smaller scale. The park also includes arguably two of the best-named natural attractions—Devil's Paint Box and Giant's Bathtub—both of which you'll explore on this hike.

Matthiessen boasts around five miles of trails and is a popular destination for visitors who come to see the beautiful Cascade Falls waterfall. Since parking is quite limited, we like to park in the less crowded River Area parking lots, which also nicely lengthens the experience. Most visitors park in the Dells lots, from which it's a straight shot to Cascade Falls.

After parking on the Vermillion River side of the park, you'll walk toward the expansive prairie grass just beyond the bathrooms and see a sign for an equestrian trail. The strenuous beginning leads over very bumpy ground, and you're dead in the sun. You'll wonder how the horses do it!

The grassy path runs for around a mile, offering pretty views of prairie grass and swooping birds. Soon you'll see forest—and shade!—and a sign for Dells Canyon. You'll dip into the trees and immediately traverse a steep rocky decline that becomes a snaky bluff trail. This portion can be tricky, with its rocky terrain and steep declines, but the bluff views and majestic oak trees projecting from the sandstone make it well worth your while.

Stay on the bluff track and eventually you'll hear the sounds of a waterfall in the distance—the signal that you're near the main attraction. You'll next reach a bridge with picturesque views of the canyon below. Many visitors stop and congregate for photos, but you'll cross the bridge and descend a set of stairs to see the Giant's Bathtub. This is a squatty waterfall that spills river water into a shallow pool. It's a fun stop, with round stone steps to hop across the water on, after which you'll continue on a trail leading deeper into the canyon.

You'll quickly notice the cooler canyon air as you continue on the path, cross another beautiful bridge, and descend a very long staircase. The canyon experience begins at the bottom of these stairs with the Devil's Paint Box, a small cove of blended sandstone and groundwater. The high levels of iron in the sandstone mixed in with the groundwater create a unique orange-brown color that is said to be reminiscent of the devil, and the mixture can stick to and paint your clothes.

As you walk toward Cascade Falls in the distance, the path widens and you can venture throughout the entire canyon area. This is an absolute joy, a sandstone fun zone. Like the canyons in Starved Rock, these sandstone formations were formed by receding glaciers. The rocks are breathtaking, and it's exciting to tunnel through caves along the edge of the canyon walls. You can also climb up the stone—if you dare—and get baptized by the rushing water of Cascade Falls. There's room behind the water to look back out into the canyon. It's truly wonderful!

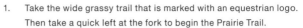

TURN-BY-TURN DIRECTIONS

1. Take the wide grassy trail that is marked with an equestrian logo. Then take a quick left at the fork to begin the Prairie Trail.
2. At 0.2 miles, stay straight at the fork.
3. At 0.8 miles, bear right to dip into some much-needed shade.
4. At 1.2 miles, stay straight at the fork.
5. At 1.7 miles, come to a fork and trail map, and stay straight to begin the Bluff Trail loop.
6. At 2.0 miles, bear left to cross the bridge; take an immediate right and head down the wooden stairs for a quick detour hike in the canyon.
7. At 2.6 miles, head up the stairs and bear left at the top to get back on the Bluff Trail.
8. At 2.8 miles, keep left to stay on the Bluff Trail.
9. At 2.9 miles, continue straight ahead.
10. At 3.0 miles, bear left down the stairs to the Lower Dells.
11. At 3.2 miles, cross the bridge and bear left on the stairs to go down into the canyon. At the bottom of the stairs, stop to visit the Devil's Paint Box just off to your right. When you're done, head north into the canyon toward Cascade Falls.
12. At 3.7 miles, arrive at Cascade Falls and stop to walk through the caves and canyon. Then turn around and head back toward the stairs.
13. At 4.0 miles, arrive at the bottom of the stairs and head back up; this time, pass the bridge and take the stairs all the way to the top. Bear right at the top.
14. At 4.5 miles, stay straight and follow the sign for River Area.
15. At 5.0 miles, bear left to get back on the Prairie Trail.
16. At 5.5 miles, bear left to stay on the Prairie Trail.
17. At 6.0 miles, bear right and return to the trailhead.

FIND THE TRAILHEAD

It's a 95-mile day-trip drive to Matthiessen State Park, roughly an hour and a half from the center of Chicago. Take IL-90/94 East for half a mile and then turn onto I-55 South. Continue for 42 miles and then take the exit for I-80 West. Stay on I-80 for 45 miles, exiting onto IL-178 toward Utica. Continue for 6.0 miles until you see the park on your right. Pass the Main Entrance and take the River Trail Entrance on your right and park in the River Area parking lot. The trailhead is just west of the public restrooms, across a road. It's not marked with its name, the Prairie Trail, but does have a sign with an equestrian logo.

TANGLED ROOTS BREWING CO.

Sharing a space with a delicious restaurant called the Lone Buffalo, one of several restaurants owned by Tangled Roots, this is a prize destination in the area. The taproom is just as dazzling as the restaurant. The brewery grows hops on a farm in Ottawa, giving its beers a "farm to foam" taste. The Devil's Paint Box IPA is a must after hiking in Matthiessen State Park. The beer is a malty, hop-forward IPA, but if you spill any it won't stain your clothes. The brewery has an exhaustive list of beers, with all sorts of styles including a red ale, a dunkelweizen, a black lager, a French Toast stout, and a good range of tropical, summery beers. The brewery and restaurant together are a big operation in a small town, and the company strongly embraces its roots in Starved Rock and Matthiessen country.

LAND MANAGER

Illinois Department of Natural Resources
Box 509
Utica, IL 61373
(815) 667-4726
www.dnr.illinois.gov/content/dam/soi/en/web/dnr/parks/documents/mattheissensitemap.pdf

BREWERY/RESTAURANT

Tangled Roots Brewing Co.
812 La Salle Street
Ottawa, IL 61350
(815) 324-9686
www.tangledrootsbrewingco.com

Distance from trailhead: 12.6 miles

THE 3 DUNE CHALLENGE

DIG IN AND CLIMB 550-FEET OF SAND

CHESTERTON, IN

▷⋯ STARTING POINT	⋯✗ DESTINATION
INDIANA DUNES NATURE CENTER	**MOUNT TOM**
🍺 BREWERY	HIKE TYPE
CHESTERTON BREWING CO.	**DIFFICULT**
🐾 DOG FRIENDLY	📅 SEASON
YES	**YEAR-ROUND**
$ FEES	⏲ DURATION
YES	**60 MIN.**
⛰ MAP REFERENCE	↦ LENGTH
TRAILHEAD	**1.6 MILES** (LOOP)
🔍 HIGHLIGHTS	〰 ELEVATION GAIN
DUNE PEAK VIEWS	**552 FEET**

4.2 %
ALCOHOL CONTENT

THIN RED LINE BLONDE ALE

 STRAW YELLOW

 FRUITY, GRAINS

 STRAWBERRY, BISCUIT

BITTERNESS

SWEETNESS

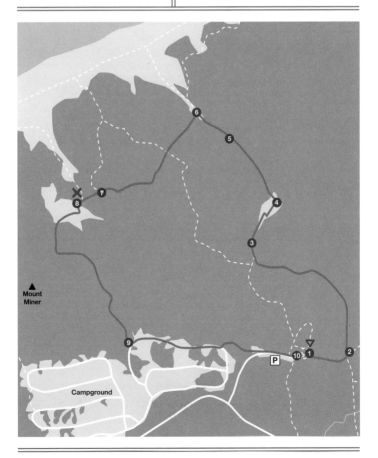

HIKE DESCRIPTION

Schedule a day trip to the Indiana Dunes and take the 3 Dune Challenge, a relentless sand climb. Then descend to Chesterton Brewery to honor a veteran with a Thin Red Line blonde ale.

The 3 Dune Challenge is not insurmountable. Walking up three connected sand dunes comes with a lot of leg burn, but it's a rewarding challenge and makes for an enjoyable hike. There are plenty of spots to rest, and the challenge is not a race.

The 3 Dune Challenge is the main attraction of Indiana Dunes State Park, more than 2,000 acres of natural area established in the 1900s. The mix of shoreline sand dunes, forest, and flora and fauna make for a unique visit.

To begin the challenge, you'll need to pay a $12 fee to enter Indiana Dunes State Park. Park at the Indiana Dunes Nature Center; the trail is right around the corner. A large well-marked trailhead announces the challenge (also called Trail 8), but the steep hill of sand ahead of you tells you all you need to know.

The first peak to climb is called Mt. Jackson and consists of 176 vertical feet of sand. This introductory hill provides a warm greeting—that is, your legs will heat up pretty quickly, aching through the deep sand at a slow but escalating pace. Mt. Jackson is for real, and deep sand is not your ordinary hiking terrain.

Luckily, about a half-mile up, the dune levels out at a nice place for a rest. You'll admire nearby jack pine and cottonwood trees as you catch your breath. At the top of Mt. Jackson, a sign informs you about who the peak was named for, how many cubic feet of sand you've walked

through (spoiler: 32 million), the maximum slope angle endured (32 degrees) and more. Each peak rewards hikers with a sign with such nuggets of trivia.

The hike gets a bit more challenging at the second dune, which has a slope of 38 degrees. You'll find it's easier to get through the deep sand if you use the dented footprints in front of you. At the top of Mt. Holden, you'll get a beautiful view of Lake Michigan. And for serious enthusiasts, there's a side trail that runs down to the water that you can jog down and run back up.

The hike continues to Mt. Tom, which begins with a twisting, forested walk. You'll follow a narrow, sandy path along steep bluffs and spot beautiful flowers like pitcher's thistle. Eventually, you'll reach the stairway to Tom—around 100 steps to the highest point, 192 feet above Lake Michigan. There's a beautiful wooden overlook deck surrounded by sand and maram grass. A good squint on a clear day will give you a view of downtown Chicago, too.

From here, there are stairs that lead you toward a twisting descent. This is now more a path and less a dreadful hill of sand, but be careful going down as you can get moving pretty fast. When at the bottom, do visit the nature center, which has an amazing bird area and delightful facts about the Indiana Dunes.

TURN-BY-TURN DIRECTIONS

1. At the trailhead in front of the nature center, head straight along the trail.
2. At 0.1 miles, bear left at the Trail 8 wooden marker.
3. At 0.4 miles, begin the climb up the first dune.
4. At 0.5 miles, arrive at the top of Mt. Jackson. Bear left at the Trail 8 marker to continue.
5. At 0.6 miles, begin the climb up the second dune.
6. At 0.7 miles, arrive at the top of Mt. Holden. Bear left to continue.
7. At 1.0 miles, begin the climb—up stairs this time—up the third dune.
8. At 1.2 miles, reach the top of Mt. Tom. Follow signs to the left and head down a new set of stairs.
9. At 1.4 miles, the trail ends at a campsite. Bear left on a park road.
10. At 1.6 miles, arrive back at the Nature Center.

FIND THE TRAILHEAD

The trailhead is at the Indiana Dunes Nature Center, 1600 North 25 E. Chesterton. (Note that there is an Indiana Dunes Visitor Center at a different location several miles away).

From downtown Chicago, take I-90 E/I-94 E for 5 miles; then stay left at the fork to continue on I-90 E, following signs for I-90 Skyway E/Indiana Toll Road for about 28 miles. Take Exit 21 for I-94/IN-51, follow signs for I-94 E/Detroit, and merge onto I-94 E. Proceed for 10 miles. Take Exit 26B onto N State Rd. 49 toward Indiana Dunes and continue straight for 1.7 miles. Then keep straight onto 25E/N State Road for 1.0 miles, entering the Indiana Dunes State Park. At the traffic circle, take the first exit onto N 25 E and continue onto County Road 100 E for 0.7 miles; then bear left into the nature center parking lot.

CHESTERTON BREWING CO.

A hike like the 3 Dune Challenge deserves a cold beer and damn fine BBQ. Chesterton Brewery has the goods, and it's even more notable for being a veteran-owned company that donates a portion of its craft-beer sales to veterans groups such as Mission One and Veterans Matter. The brewery names its beers after local servicemen and women, and the walls are adorned with photos of veterans and artworks honoring them. Chesterton Brewing has a delicious Thin Red Line blonde ale with strawberry to take the edge off. The brewery also has a blonde ale with blueberry, called Thin Blue Line. Both are smooth, low-alcohol ales that are easy on the fruit flavor and well balanced.

Vern Brown is the founder and co-owner of Chesterton Brewing and serves daily smoked BBQ meats, mac 'n' cheese, tacos, and pub fare. The beers are malt-forward and include red ales, stouts, and pale ales. Guest breweries from Illinois and Indiana are also served, broadening the brewery's offerings to more than 20 taps.

LAND MANAGER

Indiana Dunes State Park Nature Center
1600 North 25 E
Chesterton, IN 46304
(219) 926-1390
https://www.in.gov/dnr/state-parks/

BREWERY/RESTAURANT

Chesterton Brewing Co.
1050 Broadway Avenue
Chesterton, IN 46304
(219) 728-6558
www.facebook.com/TheChestertonBrewery

Distance from trailhead: 4.9 miles

WARREN DUNES STATE PARK

A TWISTING TRAIL UP A MICHIGAN SAND DUNE

SAWYER, MI

▷··· STARTING POINT	···✕ DESTINATION
MOUNT RANDALL LOOP TRAILHEAD	**MT. RANDALL PEAK**
🍺 BREWERY	♻ HIKE TYPE
GREENBUSH BREWING CO.	**STRENUOUS**
🐾 DOG FRIENDLY	📅 SEASON
YES	**YEAR-ROUND**
$ FEES	⏲ DURATION
$11 DAILY VEHICLE RECREATION PASSPORT	**1 HOUR**
⛰ MAP REFERENCE	↦ LENGTH
WWW.MICHIGAN.ORG	**1.8 MILES** (LOOP)
🔍 HIGHLIGHTS	〰 ELEVATION GAIN
RUNNING DOWN SAND HILLS	**347 FEET**

SUNSPOT
HEFEWEIZEN

 LIGHT GOLD

 LEMON,
SPICE

 DRY LEMON RIND,
CRISP

BITTERNESS   SWEETNESS

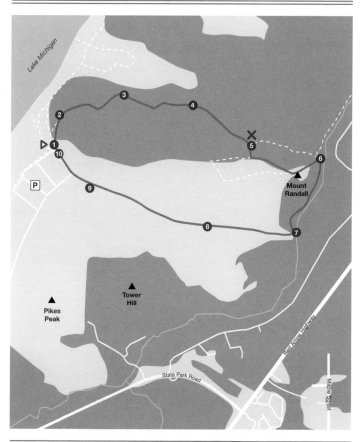

HIKE DESCRIPTION

Follow a steep woodsy trail up a sand dune, enjoy the descent, and then stop to empty the sand from your shoes at Greenbush Brewing Co. with a refreshing pint of Sunspot.

There may be a childlike glee that comes from powering up a giant hill of beach sand, but that doesn't mean it's easy. Michigan is home to a few great dunes—some more challenging than others—and one of its best is just a short ride from Chicago. Warren Dunes State Park on the shores of Lake Michigan is less than a two-hour drive from the Windy City. The park features several great trails, but the Mt. Randall Trail, which overlooks the expansive water, is particularly noteworthy.

After entering the wooded park and paying the $11 daily Recreation Passport for non-Michigan vehicles, stay straight and drive along the park road until you reach the beach. Park in the northernmost lot (there are three) and make your way to its edge, where a small sign announces the Mt. Randall Loop Trail (which combines park Trails 2 and 3). This is technically the reverse route, but doing it this way allows you to descend the sandy peak of Mt. Randall.

You'll depart from the beach and disappear into the shade of trees sprouting from a mix of sand and dirt. You'll have to skip over a few fallen trees as you make your way through this beautiful and unusual landscape. The hiking path itself is narrow and curvy, with sudden dips, turns, and inclines—you'll feel like you're walking along the thin rails of a roller coaster.

Almost three-quarters of a mile in, you'll see a steep sandhill to your right. Here, you'll have the choice of continuing along the descending path and circling the base of Mt. Randall or going up the dune. If you ask us, the only way is up! Sprint or claw your way to the top of this sandy ridge and then head left until you find yourself at the peak of Mt. Randall.

You'll know you've arrived when you suddenly feel like you're at the edge of the world, with a view of nothing but sand and sky. Tiptoe forward, inching toward the edge, and look down. What you'll see is an incredibly fun dune-side to sprint down. Let yourself go; after all, going down is always more fun.

Back on the trail, you'll come to a sign that marks the start of Trail 2. Stay the course and the path will open up to a seemingly never-ending stretch of sand and a few smaller dunes to climb. You can also continue along Trail 2 to arrive back at the parking lot and the beach. Lastly, there's no better way to wash off the sand than with a dip in the icy waters of Lake Michigan.

TURN-BY-TURN DIRECTIONS

1. At the Mt. Randall Trailhead, head straight to start the hike, which begins with Trail 3.
2. At 0.1 miles, stay straight at the Trail 3 marker.
3. At 0.3 miles, reach an intersection with another trail; stay straight at the Trail 3 marker.
4. At 0.5 miles, stay straight to keep following Trail 3.
5. At 0.7 miles, head right for a steep shortcut to the top of Mt. Randall.
6. At 1.0 miles, descend a very steep dune hill to get back on Trail 3.
7. At 1.1 miles, come to a trailhead and parking lot; take a sharp right to begin on Trail 2 and continue the Mt. Randall Loop Trail.
8. At 1.4 miles, climb a bunny hill to stay on Trail 2.
9. At 1.7 miles, climb down the bunny hill.
10. At 1.8 miles, finish the trail, which ends in the beach parking lot where it began.

FIND THE TRAILHEAD

From Chicago, it takes around an hour and a half to drive to Sawyer, Michigan. You'll start on I-90 East, following signs to merge onto Interstate 90 Skyway East/Indiana Toll Road. From the Indiana Toll Road, merge onto I-94 East; stay on it for 43 miles and into Michigan. To get to the park, take Exit 12 toward Sawyer Road. In a little over a mile, turn left onto State Park Road. In another mile, the park will be on your left. Once inside Warren Dunes State Park, you'll drive toward the beach and park in the northernmost parking lot (there are three large lots along the beach).

GREENBUSH BREWING CO.

Sawyer, Michigan and its surrounding summer resort towns have experienced a boom in breweries over the last few years, but it all began with Greenbush. The brewery started as a small brick taproom lined with glass mugs but has since expanded to include a neighboring sitting room (designed to look like an old diner) and a market area selling beer and meats and cheeses. Sunspot is a stalwart hefeweizen and the perfect way to rehydrate after a day in the sand and sun. The beer's beachy flavor, with notes of cloves and lemon, nicely complements a hike through the dunes. The brewery debuted the beer as a summer seasonal many years ago, but it was so popular that it can now be found on tap year-round. It's also notable that the brewery serves tremendous food, which is why the diner-themed addition fits so well. A range of deli sandwiches are on the extensive menu, as are BBQ platters of brisket, pulled pork, and chicken. Popular are the massive helpings of custom mac and cheese (throw in the brisket) and Joique Wings, jerk-rubbed chicken wings tossed in a Joique sauce. You can buy these wings to cook at home, too.

LAND MANAGER

Warren Dunes State Park
12032 Red Arrow Highway,
Sawyer, MI 49125
(269) 426-4013
www.michigan.org/property/warren-dunes-state-park

BREWERY/RESTAURANT

Greenbush Brewing Co.
5885 Sawyer Road
Sawyer, MI 49125
(269) 405-1076
www.greenbushbrewing.com

Distance from trailhead: 3.3 miles

DEDICATION AND ACKNOWLEDGEMENTS

First and foremost, we would like to thank our families and friends for all the love and support we received while working on this book. It may have seemed like we were in hiding every weekend for several months, but we were just hiking. Thank you for championing us.

We especially want to thank our son Selden for being a trooper and going on nearly every one of these hikes, trudging up dunes and swatting off ticks. Thank you for making us laugh at the breweries, even though you don't like the smell of beer being brewed. Surely, after all the places we visited this year, you'll one day be able to write a book about the breweries with the best French fries and Wi-Fi signals.

We also want to give a major shout-out to our dear friend Bryan Barker, who joined us on many of the hikes. He helped us troubleshoot map issues, kept us entertained, and brought his fierce foosball game to the taprooms.

Thank you to Linda Sedgwick for all of your support and for hanging out with our son for a few weekends so we could knock out some of the longer hikes child-free. And thank you to Ron Ochwat and the Austin family—Lori, Bob, Tom, Matt, Nick, and Jacob—for taking care of our dog Finn.

We'd also like to thank the polite staff members at each brewery and all the park employees we encountered. We appreciate your guidance and the time you spent answering our questions. We enjoyed getting to know you, even if in secret!

Of course, this book owes much to the amazing work of Sonia Curtis and the Helvetiq team. Sonia's intuitive, instinctual, and intelligent edits elevated the book, and we thank her for her patience as we juggled jobs and worked weekends and nights. Thank you dearly to Helvetiq for the opportunity to bring this series to Chicago. We hope the city's charm shines through!

Lastly, huge thanks to everyone who supports this book going forward—friends promoting the book, booksellers carrying the book, breweries sharing the book—and thank you Chicago! We love you. We hope people enjoy this book, their hikes, and their beers!

Cheers,
Dan and Jessica